Moodle Course Design Best Practices

Learn the best practices to design and develop interactive and highly effective Moodle courses

Susan Smith Nash

Michelle Moore

[PACKT] open source ✳

PUBLISHING   community experience distilled

BIRMINGHAM - MUMBAI

About the Authors

Susan Smith Nash, who has been involved in the design, development, and administration of e-Learning programs and courses since earning her Ph.D. in the late 1990s, has developed and administered online courses on many platforms, using many different learning management systems. She is responsible for developing degree and certificate programs delivered in online and hybrid formats and has worked on implementing e-Learning in universities, corporations, and associations.

The author of the award-winning e-Learning blog *E-Learning Queen* and several books on e-Learning, Susan Smith Nash has focused on developing courses that optimize user experience and enhance performance, outcomes, and course persistence/completion.

Her portfolio of publications includes peer-reviewed articles and books, including the following:

- The video *Moodle for Training and Professional Development*, *Packt Publishing*, 2013
- The book *E-Learning Success: From Courses to Careers*, *Texture Press*, 2012
- The book *E-Learner Survival Guide*, *Texture Press*, 2011
- The book *Moodle 1.9 Teaching Techniques*, *Packt Publishing*, 2010

I would like to express my most profound appreciation to the reviewers of the chapters: Diana Benner, Rafael Reyna Camones, Anna Krassa, and Danny Wahl. They took the time to prepare careful, thoughtful, and thorough reviews that were always right on target and extremely helpful.

I would also like to thank Elaine Bontempi, Ph.D., whose expertise in instructional design and instructional psychology has been invaluable for coming up with the best ways to develop effective and motivating courses.

It has been a pleasure to work with the Packt Publishing editorial team: Aboli Ambardekar and Amey Varangaonkar. Their professionalism and promptness as well as their solution-centered orientation has made this project a great experience.

Michelle Moore, a former middle school math teacher, has been an advocate for Moodle since discovering it more than ten years ago during the writing of a review of learning management systems while completing her master's degree in Instructional Design and Technology. Enamored with Moodle's capabilities and its foundation in social constructionism, it wasn't long before Michelle's passion led her to a full-time position in training and providing support for educators and trainers in schools, universities, and businesses across North America. Since then, Michelle has helped thousands of Moodlers leverage Moodle's features to design quality online, blended, and mobile learning experiences.

Michelle is an energetic, award-winning speaker who presents regularly at MoodleMoots and educational technology conferences worldwide on the use of Moodle, with a strong emphasis on pedagogy and best practices. Michelle is pursuing a doctorate in Learning Technologies at the University of North Texas where she is actively researching online education and constructivist teaching methods. Follow Michelle on Twitter at @michelledmoore or visit her blog at http://moodleandmoore.com.

I would first like to thank the many Moodlers who have been so willing to share, experiment, and learn with me; without them, this book would not have been possible. I am also indebted to Bryan Williams who gave me the opportunity to turn my passion for Moodle into a career. To Susan, my co-author, thank you for being my personal cheerleader and going the extra mile to make this book a reality.

I would also like to thank Dr. Bill Elieson, my mentor at UNT, for his ongoing support and advice. Last, but definitely not least, I must thank my husband, Jonathan, for first exposing me to the concept of open source software so many years ago. We make a great team and I look forward to seeing what the future holds!

About the Reviewers

Diana Benner, an educator and technologist for over 15 years, is currently a technology administrator in the State of Texas. She regularly shares her knowledge of online learning through webinars and presentations at both national and state technology conferences.

She has administered Moodle for a large K-12 public school district as well as designed and facilitated many online professional learning courses for educators. She worked as an online learning specialist, where she would train educators in the use of Moodle as well as provide technical support. In addition, as an instructional designer for the State of Texas, she had the opportunity to create SCORM-based e-Learning courses in Moodle. She has a Master of Education degree in Educational Technology and has received her Online Course Instructors certification, which certifies her to teach online and develop online courses. She is an active member of the Texas Computer Education Association (TCEA) and the Texas Distance Learning Association (TxDLA).

She enjoys training others on the process of translating traditional content to the online environment. Diana currently resides in Austin, Texas and can be contacted for consultation at diana.benner@gmail.com. Her online portfolio can be found at http://dbenner.org.

I would like to thank my family and friends for their unconditional support. I would also like to thank Packt Publishing for giving me the opportunity to review this book. In addition, I am grateful to my colleague, Miguel Guhlin, for not only introducing me to Moodle but also continually inspiring me to learn more about educational technologies and most importantly, for making me realize the value of sharing what I'm learning.

Rafael Reyna Camones is a consultant for information technology. He has experience in the development of modules for Moodle and focuses on the integration of the e-Learning platform with mobile devices (iOS, Android, and Windows Phone).

He graduated as Systems Engineer from the Universidad Nacional José Faustino Sánchez Carrión. He has trained university staff in the use of Moodle and developed a pilot manner for implementing the courses. In his spare time, he enjoys a good conversation and exchanging ideas.

Another book reviewed by Rafael Reyna Camones is the Instant book *Moodle Quiz Module How-to*, *Packt Publishing*.

Anna Krassa (kanna) has a bachelor's degree in Librarianship and Information Science, but is working mostly as an e-Learning consultant. She is located in North Greece (Nea Moudania, Chalkidiki) and became the first Moodle-certified teacher in Greece in December 2006. In May 2007, she became a Mentor-assessor for MTC/MCCC candidates, collaborating with HRD New Zealand Moodle Partner—Certification Central Administration. From 2012, Anna became the main Mentor-assessor in the MCCC Central Administration. Her responsibilities include assessing MCCC candidates, mentoring MCCC Mentor-assessors, and representing HRDNZ (Moodle Partner) in conferences.

Anna has also been working with the GAC Corporate Academy since 2007, initially as an external facilitator from HRDNZ Moodle Partner facilitating the Personal and Professional Development course. When the course withdrew after two years, her position changed from facilitating to course development and GAClearn administration because of her Moodle background. Since 2012, she has been working as a GCA Learning Developer. Her responsibilities include site administration, course design, facilitator training and support, participant assistance, research on e-Learning and Moodle, as well as representation of GCA in conferences, seminars, and similar events.

In Greece, she has worked for the e-Learning service of the Greek School Network and Telemathea, the Library of University of Macedonia. As a volunteer, she has worked for FreeMoodle and Mathisis, the most active e-schools in Greece and Cyprus. Internationally, she has worked in her capacity as HRDNZ contractor in Bahrain (GII Academy), Ethiopia (Mekelle University), Canada (Northern Alberta Institute of Technology), and Cyprus (European University of Cyprus).

Anna started collaborating with Packt Publishing as a technical reviewer in 2013. So far, she has reviewed the following books:

- *Moodle 2.5 Multimedia*, *João Pedro Soares Fernandes*
- *Moodle Course Design Best Practices*, *Susan Smith Nash* and *Michelle Moore*

On a personal level, she is married to Vasilis and together they have a lovely daughter.

Danny Wahl is an educational technology consultant and implementation specialist working in the Asia-Pacific region with a particular focus on international schools. He has assisted several schools with 1:1 computing and online and mobile learning programs, among other things. When he is not working, he enjoys web development, studying the Bible, and playing the ukulele.

www.PacktPub.com

Support files, eBooks, discount offers and more

You might want to visit www.PacktPub.com for support files and downloads related to your book.

Did you know that Packt offers eBook versions of every book published, with PDF and ePub files available? You can upgrade to the eBook version at www.PacktPub.com and as a print book customer, you are entitled to a discount on the eBook copy. Get in touch with us at service@packtpub.com for more details.

At www.PacktPub.com, you can also read a collection of free technical articles, sign up for a range of free newsletters and receive exclusive discounts and offers on Packt books and eBooks.

http://PacktLib.PacktPub.com

Do you need instant solutions to your IT questions? PacktLib is Packt's online digital book library. Here, you can access, read and search across Packt's entire library of books.

Why Subscribe?

- Fully searchable across every book published by Packt
- Copy and paste, print and bookmark content
- On demand and accessible via web browser

Free Access for Packt account holders

If you have an account with Packt at www.PacktPub.com, you can use this to access PacktLib today and view nine entirely free books. Simply use your login credentials for immediate access.

Table of Contents

Preface

Moodle is a very flexible learning management system that is open source and used by millions of people around the world to host and offer online education and training programs. Moodle is an open source learning management system with a wide array of contributed activities, themes, and resources that developers make available for free.

A vast array of Moodle resources often causes difficulties such that it is not easy to take advantage of so many applications and design options. However, now you can overcome these limitations; *Moodle Course Design Best Practices* helps you put those resources to good use and create Moodle courses that are ideal for all kinds of organizations, teachers, and learners.

In this book, you'll learn the best practices to create effective and engaging courses for all kinds of learning organizations, ranging from online schools to colleges, universities, training centers, and even online communities.

You'll learn how to plan the structure of your courses, select the best resources, activities, and assessments for your purposes, and use the latest Moodle-friendly programs, plugins, applications, and social media.

We hope you will enjoy this book and find it to be both useful and helpful.

What this book covers

With the information in the chapters, you'll be able to work with Moodle from the very beginning and have the information you need at every step of the way.

Chapter 1, *Preparing to Build an Exemplary Moodle Course*, shows what you need to do if you're setting up your first Moodle course. It also contains information about where to go for information and support.

Chapter 2, *Planning Your Course*, explains how to develop a course that incorporates learning theories by showing you how to build good learning objectives. You will also learn the best approaches to plan your course so that you can structure it to maximize the chances of success.

Chapter 3, *Organizing Your Course*, focuses on course organization and shows you how to choose the right course format, and define course settings.

Chapter 4, *Best Practices in Content Delivery*, discusses how to manage content and the best approaches to deliver content of all kinds.

Chapter 5, *Designing Self-paced Independent Study Courses*, shows you how to design and structure self-paced independent study courses and where to put all the materials, assessments, and other items. It also discusses how to build a course that motivates students and encourages them to complete it.

Chapter 6, *Developing Cohort-based Courses with Teacher-student Interaction*, focuses on the best design for instructor-led courses that are meant to be delivered to groups of students. It discusses the best themes to use and then reviews the theme settings for a course and its ideal format as well as the best resources and activities to use and how to use them.

Chapter 7, *Creating Student-centered Project-based Courses*, helps you create courses that include student projects and collaborative activities. It demonstrates which universal and course-specific theme settings are best for your course, and how to select the ideal combination of resources, activities, and assessments.

Chapter 8, *Moodle for Online Communities*, focuses on how Moodle can be used for online communities, either closed, as in the case of specific organizations, or open, as in the case of social media. It includes strategies for motivating students and discusses how to organize Moodle to take advantage of the constantly changing landscape of the social media, programs, applications, resources, and activities that are available for Moodle.

What you need for this book

You will need to have access to an installation of Moodle 2.0 or newer (ideally Version 2.6 or newer), and you will need to install the latest versions of Java and JavaScript. In addition, you may want Adobe Reader and Adobe Acrobat so that you can create PDF documents. It would also be helpful to use an audio-editing program, such as Audacity, and an image editor, such as PicMonkey or Pixlr.

Who this book is for

This book is for teachers, trainers, course creators, instructional technologists, instructional designers, and Moodle administrators.

Conventions

In this book, you will find a number of styles of text that distinguish between different kinds of information. Here are some examples of these styles, and an explanation of their meaning.

Code words in text, database table names, folder names, filenames, file extensions, pathnames, dummy URLs, user input, and Twitter handles are shown as follows: "suppose you have a file in your course called Course Guide and wish to refer your students to that guide".

New terms and **important words** are shown in bold. Words that you see on the screen, in menus, or dialog boxes for example, appear in the text like this: "Go to the **NAVIGATION** block."

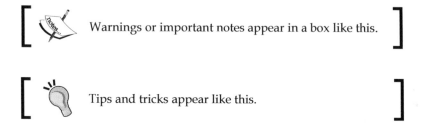

Warnings or important notes appear in a box like this.

Tips and tricks appear like this.

Reader feedback

Feedback from our readers is always welcome. Let us know what you think about this book—what you liked or may have disliked. Reader feedback is important for us to develop titles that you really get the most out of.

To send us general feedback, simply send an e-mail to feedback@packtpub.com, and mention the book title via the subject of your message.

If there is a topic that you have expertise in and you are interested in either writing or contributing to a book, see our author guide on www.packtpub.com/authors.

Customer support

Now that you are the proud owner of a Packt book, we have a number of things to help you to get the most from your purchase.

Errata

Although we have taken every care to ensure the accuracy of our content, mistakes do happen. If you find a mistake in one of our books—maybe a mistake in the text or the code—we would be grateful if you would report this to us. By doing so, you can save other readers from frustration and help us improve subsequent versions of this book. If you find any errata, please report them by visiting http://www.packtpub.com/submit-errata, selecting your book, clicking on the **errata submission form** link, and entering the details of your errata. Once your errata are verified, your submission will be accepted and the errata will be uploaded on our website, or added to any list of existing errata, under the Errata section of that title. Any existing errata can be viewed by selecting your title from http://www.packtpub.com/support.

Piracy

Piracy of copyright material on the Internet is an ongoing problem across all media. At Packt, we take the protection of our copyright and licenses very seriously. If you come across any illegal copies of our works, in any form, on the Internet, please provide us with the location address or website name immediately so that we can pursue a remedy.

Please contact us at copyright@packtpub.com with a link to the suspected pirated material.

We appreciate your help in protecting our authors, and our ability to bring you valuable content.

Questions

You can contact us at questions@packtpub.com if you are having a problem with any aspect of the book, and we will do our best to address it.

1

Preparing to Build an Exemplary Moodle Course

So, you would like to build a great Moodle course? Or maybe improve the one you have? You've come to the right place. We want to help you take full advantage of all that Moodle has to offer, while creating more engaging and user-friendly experiences for your learners. At the same time, we want to make sure that you're not working harder than you need to be. We'll help you avoid doing things the hard way and focus your efforts so you're spending time where it will have the most impact.

Well-designed Moodle courses encompass much more than what happens in the course shell. The course design process begins with an optimally configured Moodle site and an understanding of the opportunities afforded by the Moodle platform.

In this chapter, we'll discuss:

- The advantages of Moodle from the perspective of a course designer
- Resources available to support you as you set up your Moodle site
- Site settings needed to implement the ideas presented later in the book

The advantages of Moodle

We'll start with the question, "Why Moodle?" What does it have to offer course designers, trainers, and educators? First and foremost, as educators ourselves, the fact that Moodle is built around an instructional ideal or educational philosophy makes it pretty exceptional. More specifically, Moodle's design is driven by a social constructionist pedagogy as inspired by educational theorists such as Vygotsky, Papert, and others. Social constructionism is a view of education that relies on the belief that people create knowledge through the process of constructing artifacts, including text, media, or other such projects, within a social environment. In short, this means that the creator of Moodle, Martin Dougiamas, built Moodle based on the idea that people learn best when they have an opportunity to construct, share, collaborate with, and learn from others. As we discuss Moodle's features, we'll see many ways in which this philosophy is exhibited.

 You can learn more about the pedagogy and philosophy behind Moodle in Moodle Docs, the Moodle Documentation wiki at http://docs.moodle.org/en/Pedagogy and http://docs.moodle.org/en/Philosophy.

Despite a strong pedagogical foundation, Moodle doesn't lock you into one way of teaching, which is another advantage of Moodle. It offers an array of choices when it comes to how you construct and deliver your course. In fact, we use this flexibility as the foundation for how this book is organized, with chapters devoted to a few of the more common ways that Moodle is used. Some are heavily reliant on social constructionist strategies, and others, less so. If you want to create a self-paced, content-driven course, Moodle can do that. If you need to facilitate a cohort-based, student-centered course, Moodle can do that too. Likewise, if you want to offer a very structured, linear course or, at the opposite end of the spectrum, manage a community, we think you'll find Moodle to be accommodating.

Getting started with Moodle

To make the most of this book, you'll need to have access in the role of a teacher (as a minimum). In this role, you'll have the ability to add and edit activities and resources so you can experiment with the ideas presented. Having site administrator permissions is helpful, but not required.

If you don't currently have access to a Moodle site, or lack course editing privileges, then you have several options. We can't describe every option in detail, but we can guide you towards the resources to assist you in filling in the gaps.

The first option is to outsource the setup and hosting of your Moodle site. If you don't have experience setting up and managing web servers but need your Moodle site to be available on the Web, then this choice is probably the best for you. The Moodle Docs website offers a comprehensive discussion related to selecting hosting services at `http://docs.moodle.org/en/Finding_and_Selecting_A_Web_Host`. The best choice for you, as this page outlines, will depend on your level of experience in managing servers and with Moodle or other learning management systems. It's also necessary to weigh factors such as cost and the level of Moodle support you prefer. We recommend seeking out a Moodle Partner as they are certified service providers with a high level of expertise and experience. In addition, each Moodle Partner contributes a percentage of their revenue to Moodle Headquarters that, in turn, is used to compensate the developers who bring Moodle to life.

The second option is to install your own Moodle site on either your own server or on a hosted platform. For complete instructions, Moodle Docs again has a great resource that can be found on the *Installing Moodle* page at `http://docs.moodle.org/en/ Installing_Moodle`.

There are advantages and disadvantages to setting up and managing a site on your own, but doing so is a good fit for some. For example, the out-of-pocket cost will generally be less if you set up and manage your own site, but you may spend more time seeking out solutions on your own. You'll also likely have more freedom and flexibility when it comes to installing plugins or making code modifications, but even though it is a nice feature, you run the risk of doing it incorrectly. Another disadvantage of setting up and managing a site on your own is that you may be constrained by size. If your organization has a large number of courses, with a large number of users, it may be too time consuming to try to do everything on your own. Moodle updates and upgrades quite often, and plugins are also changed regularly. It is time consuming enough to manage your courses and users without having to worry about Moodle updates and plugin upgrades.

If you're just looking to experiment with Moodle and don't need to make your site available to others, you might like the local install option. With the local install, you basically set up a Moodle server on your personal computer. The advantage of this option is that you have a fully functioning Moodle site that you have complete control over. Furthermore, it's easy to set up and there's little risk of butchering your entire organization's courses and losing data if you wish to experiment. Further, if at some point you like what you've created, you can transfer individual courses or the site as a whole to a site hosted on the web.

The biggest downside to this arrangement is that since the site will not be publicly available, it'll be more difficult to share what you've done or involve others with testing.

> For the local install, you can choose from Mac or Windows packages. The Windows package is available at `http://download.moodle.org/windows/`, and the Mac version can be found at `http://download.moodle.org/macosx/`. Regardless of which platform you use, you'll want to install the most recent stable version (that is, **MOODLE_26_STABLE**). The development version can be fun, but you're more likely to encounter bugs. The Linux version can be found at `http://docs.moodle.org/26/en/RedHat_Linux_installation`.

Finally, there are a number of free Moodle hosting options available. These often restrict you to a single course or limit administrator permissions, but can be a fine choice for someone who is getting started. Though in most cases you'll have less control than afforded by a local install, these options do offer the advantage of allowing you to make your course available to others.

> You can find the complete list of free Moodle hosting providers at `http://docs.moodle.org/en/Free_Moodle`.

Preparing your Moodle workspace

If you have just established your first Moodle site, then there are a few things you'll need to prepare for the activities in the coming chapters. If you are working with an existing Moodle site, you may want to review the information presented here just to make sure you have everything you need to follow along. If you are a teacher and unable to create additional accounts, never fear, as Moodle offers the **Switch role to...** feature that allows you to view course activities from the student's perspective.

You will have to complete the following tasks:

1. Create at least two user accounts, one to be assigned the role of teacher and the other to be assigned the role of student.
2. Create a new course shell for development and testing.
3. Assign roles within the new course shell to the accounts created in the first step.

Now, rather than repeating the detailed administrator documentation that abounds on the Web and in print, we will just direct you to the appropriate option in the **ADMINISTRATION** block for each activity listed here. We will also provide links to related documentation. For a more in-depth discussion of these administrative tasks and others, we encourage you to invest in training designed for Moodle Administrators. One example is the book *Moodle 2 Administration* by Alex Büchner as a comprehensive guide.

Creating user accounts

To create your two user accounts, go to the **Site administration** menu, which is on the left-hand side of the screen by default, and click on **Add a new user** after navigating to **Users | Accounts**. Then, enter the required information for the new user account and click on **Create user**.

Find documentation for this at `http://docs.moodle.org/en/Add_a_new_user`, or if in doubt, accepting the default setting is acceptable too.

Creating a new course shell

Now, let's create a course shell so that our new users can participate in a course by performing the following steps:

1. Go to the **NAVIGATION** block.
2. Click on **Courses**.
3. Click on the **Add a new course** button.
4. Enter the required information for your new course.
5. Click on **Save changes**.

We'll revisit many of the course settings as we begin to work on the design of your course, but if you'd like more information in the meantime, you can find it at `http://docs.moodle.org/26/en/Course_settings`.

Assigning course roles

When you've finished creating your course shell, you'll be prompted to enroll users in the course. Go to the **ADMINISTRATION** block, then go to **Course administration**, and then navigate to **Users | Enrolled users**. To assign course roles, perform the following steps:

1. To add or enroll your teacher account, click on the **Enrol users** button.
2. Choose **Teacher** from the list of roles at the top of the screen.

3. Click on the **Enrol** button to the right of your teacher account to complete the process.

4. Click on **Finish enrolling users** to close the window. Repeat the process for your student account with the role set to **Student**.

Site settings for course designers

Before we move our discussion to the specifics of Moodle course design and into that newly created course shell, we want to spend some more time in the **Site administration** menu. For those who have site administrator access, fantastic! You'll be able to review the suggestions that follow and change settings at will. If you don't have administrator permissions, don't walk away just yet! Our goal here is to provide you with recommendations you can take to your Moodle administrator.

If you've not had a chance to explore the **Site administration** menu, you should know first that while there are lots of "techie" settings, there are also many less technical settings that impact how the site works for course designers, teachers, and students. In fact, we would propose that for any Moodle site, make sure that at least two people review the site settings: first, an system administrator who is focused on the technical needs, and second, an instructional technologist who is focused on the settings that impact those delivering and receiving instruction.

In this section, we'll present our recommendations for a few of the most broadly applicable instructional settings, along with a list of other settings that we encourage you to explore and consider in light of your organization's unique needs.

You will have to complete the following tasks:

1. Activate filters so that certain items, such as links and videos, will automatically appear in your course.

2. Enable completion tracking so that students can keep track of their pace in your course.

3. Enable conditional activities so that students complete one assignment before moving on to another.

Activating filters

First on the list of administration settings for the course creators are filters. In nontechnical terms, filters scan what you write and apply rules to make neat things happen, such as automatically creating links or embedding media.

To see a complete list of available filters, go to the **Site administration** menu and then to **Plugins | Filters | Manage filters**. You will see a page similar to the following screenshot:

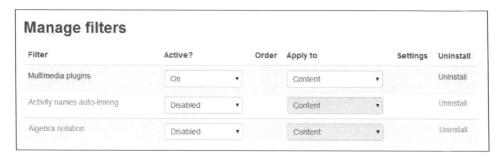

On this page, we recommend enabling, or turning on, the following filters:

- **Activity names auto-linking**
- **Glossary auto-linking**
- **Multimedia plugins**

As suggested by their names, the **Activity names auto-linking** and **Glossary auto-linking** filters offer similar functionality. The **Activity names auto-linking** filter automatically creates links to activities when the name of the activity is mentioned elsewhere in the course. For example, suppose you have a file in your course called `Course Guide` and wish to refer your students to that guide in a forum post. Without autolinking enabled, you will need to copy the link to the guide to include it in your post. With autolinking, however, as long as you type the name of the file or activity exactly as it's named in the course, Moodle will automatically generate the link for you. Not only is this autolinking feature a time saver for you, but it also improves usability and navigation for students. The following screenshot explains about the link generated for the file `Course Guide`:

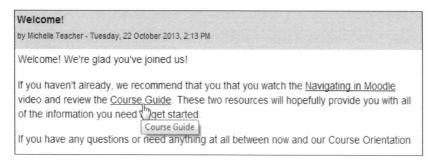

Your automatically generated links may not look exactly like those shown in the previous screenshot. The appearance is dependent on the theme being used on your site. In many themes, the linked word or phrase is highlighted with a gray background.

Glossary auto-linking automatically creates links to entries in the course glossary when the terms are used elsewhere in the course. So, if students are working through course content or even reading forum posts and see an unfamiliar word, they can quickly click on the link and have the definition for it at their fingertips. Better yet, these filters work on the content generated by the students as well as on the content created by the teacher.

 A word of caution for those with existing Moodle sites

Be sure to forewarn other teachers and course designers before you turn on autolinking because doing so may result in unintended links. Links to glossary terms suddenly appearing in a quiz may be of particular concern. Realize, of course, that these filters can be disabled at the course level and even in quizzes, but it's better to make teachers aware of this in advance. Finally, instead of setting these filters to **On**, you could choose to set them to **Off** but have them available and allow teachers to turn them on at will.

The **Multimedia plugins** filter, also on this **Manage filters** page, should be enabled. The **Multimedia plugins** filter recognizes links to multimedia files, such as .mp3, .mp4, or .mov files, and presents the appropriate player automatically. With this filter, if you link a .mp3 file, an audio player will automatically be displayed, allowing students to play the file instead of downloading it.

 For more information about these and other available filters, visit http://docs.moodle.org/en/Managing_filters.

Enabling completion tracking

Completion tracking and conditional activities were introduced in the Moodle 2.0 release and were quickly added to our list of features to enable. The completion tracking and conditional activities features allow you to turn the course page into a checklist for your students. When incorporated at the course level, a checkbox will appear next to each activity, which the student can then mark as complete as they finish the task or view the content. This feature helps the students stay on track in the course and can be very motivating.

The following screenshot shows sample checkboxes next to their respective task:

Completion tracking is flexible. You can set criteria, such as when a student submits an assignment or posts a specified number of replies within a forum. When the performance criteria have been satisfied, the application automatically indicates task completion. This feature makes it much easier for students to keep track of their place in the course.

To enable completion tracking, perform the following steps:

1. Go to the **Site administration** menu and select **Advanced features**.
2. Scroll down the **Advanced features** page until you find **Enable completion tracking**.
3. Check the box next to it to enable it.
4. Click on the **Save changes** button at the bottom of the page.

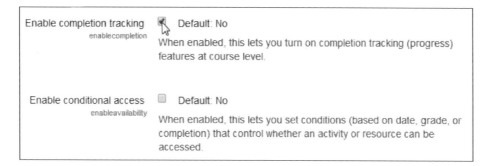

 Read more about completion tracking on the Moodle Docs website at http://docs.moodle.org/en/Activity_completion.

Enabling conditional activities

The conditional activities feature makes it possible for a teacher or course designer to limit access to activities or resources based on defined criteria or conditions. For example, you can require that a student complete a lesson before seeing a quiz as shown in the following screenshot:

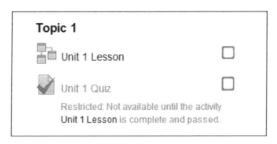

This feature can also be used to tailor instructions to the performance of individual learners or to add game-like components to your Moodle course. This feature offers many possibilities; to learn more, visit `http://docs.moodle.org/en/Conditional_activities`.

Enable the conditional activities setting just below the setting for completion tracking by performing the following steps:

1. Go to the **Site administration** menu and choose **Advanced features**.
2. Scroll down the **Advanced features** page until you find **Enable conditional access**.
3. Check the box next to it to enable it.
4. Click on the **Save changes** button at the bottom of the page.

Summary

In this chapter, we've laid the groundwork for an exceptional, well-designed Moodle course. We first reviewed options and resources for setting up your Moodle site. Then, we created user accounts and a course to use for the activities in the coming chapters. Last but not least, we changed a few important settings in the **Site administration** menu to provide additional functionality for our courses.

In the next chapter, we will take a step back and focus on learning theory and instructional design concepts that will guide you through planning the structure of your course. In doing so, you will learn how to align the course design with your overall learning objectives. We'll also consider the kinds of assessments you will administer in order to evaluate whether or not the learning goals have been met.

2
Planning Your Course

In the previous chapter, we reviewed the basics of Moodle and learned how to get started with site-wide settings and configurations. Now, we will take a step back and review the basics of pedagogy and instructional design. They are important as you set up your educational programs and build courses in Moodle. If you fail to take pedagogy and instructional design into consideration early in the process, you run the risk of having to rebuild your courses later, which can be very tedious, time consuming, and expensive (in terms of labor). So, it's a great idea to bookmark this chapter and return to it often, each time you begin to develop a new program, course template, demo course, or individual courses.

Let's start with a fundamental question: what would you like your students to be able to do after they complete your course?

It sounds like a simple question, but it's the key to setting up an effective structure for your Moodle course and also to select the best possible resources, activities, and assessments.

As you plan your course, it is important to keep in mind what you want your students to learn, and then, how you would like them to demonstrate their skills and knowledge. With these things in mind, you can plan your course so that it has a clear, logical structure and the elements tie neatly together and reinforce each other.

We'll learn how to use course-level learning outcomes as the foundation for your course. Using course-level learning outcomes, we're starting with the "big picture" view. Then, we'll take a closer look at each of the sections in your course and learn how to create more specific learning outcomes that will serve as the framework that ties the big-picture goals to the resources, activities, and assessments of your course. With such a solid foundation and framework, you'll never feel lost or frustrated as you build your course. Instead, you'll feel confident as you select your course's resources, activities, and assessments.

In this chapter, we'll discuss the following topics:

- Writing and using learning outcomes spanning the course
- The importance of outlining learning outcomes
- Ideal course structure
- Universal Design for Learning
- Resources and activities selection
- Effective assessment strategies

Learning outcomes

One of the best ways to start planning your course is by thinking about what you'd like your students to be able to do when they successfully complete it. At the same time, it is good to envision how they should demonstrate their new knowledge or skill. What your students are able to do as a result of taking the course are the learning outcomes of the course. Both terms refer to the notion of a course, that is, focuses not just on the content to be covered, but also on the skills, abilities, beliefs, and attitudes that result upon completion of the course.

Learning outcomes encompass the knowledge, skills, and abilities that the students should gain on completing the course. Learning outcomes are known by other terms as well. They are often referred to as course outcomes, course objectives, learning objectives, and student learning outcomes. In all cases, they are important because they shape every aspect of your course, from selecting content and activities to creating assessments that determine whether or not the course or learning program was effective.

You can learn more about learning outcomes in the *Tips on Writing Learning Outcomes* section at the University Library page of the University of Illinois at Urbana-Champaign website. Visit this section at http://www.library.illinois.edu/infolit/learningoutcomes.html.

As you consider what you would like your students to do, you are incorporating a student-centric approach that puts more emphasis on *how* they should do something than *what* they should do, which results in a more active approach. Instead of thinking about what you'd like to teach, you're considering how to facilitate the learning process.

Writing learning outcomes

Because you are focusing on student performance and bearing in mind what you'd like your students to do and how they should be able to demonstrate their new knowledge, skills, and abilities, your outcomes need to be written with the plan of action in mind.

So, as you go through the process of determining what the learning outcomes should be for your course, jot them down. You may come up with a long list, but later, make sure that you select the ones that best reflect what you'd like your students to achieve. We'd like to follow best practices for instructional design, so we recommend that your final list should contain not more than six or seven outcomes.

You can learn more about best practices for developing learning and performance outcomes in the classic work *The Systematic Design of Instruction* by Walter Dick and Lou Cary in 1978. Their work was so influential that it came to be known as the Dick and Carey Systems Approach Model and was widely adopted by instructional designers and training developers. For an overview of the Dick and Carey Systems Approach Model, you may visit the **Big Dog & Little Dog's Performance Juxtaposition** page at http://www.nwlink.com/~donclark/history_isd/carey.html.

To transform your informal list of desired outcomes to formal learning outcomes statements, you may benefit from using the S. M. A. R. T. approach, which was first developed by George T. Doran in the November, 1981 issue of *Management Review*. Since it was first published, it has become very popular in many applications that need to measure goals and outcomes. The criteria are very handy for making sure that your statements are complete. Here are the S. M. A. R. T. guidelines, where your outcomes should be as follows:

- **Specific**: Make sure that the desired outcomes are not too broad
- **Measurable**: Include a quantity or a way to measure progress
- **Attainable**: Your desired outcomes need to be achievable
- **Relevant**: Make sure that the desired outcomes relate to your course
- **Time bound**: Make it clear by when the objective should be achieved

As you write your S. M. A. R. T. outcomes, be sure to avoid verbs or phrases such as "understand", "appreciate", "know about", "familiarize yourself with", and "develop an awareness of". Instead, use active verbs and phrases that connote measurable results, such as "identify", "describe", "analyze", "evaluate", and "create". Look back at the guidelines, and you'll see that they may not be measurable and may also have other deficiencies.

Bloom's Taxonomy

As you start to shape your learning outcomes, many teachers and course designers find it very useful to use Bloom's Taxonomy as a guide. Benjamin Bloom was an educational psychologist who helped develop a classification scheme for learning objectives that reflects how to show mastery in different skills, knowledge areas, and abilities.

The result—Bloom's Taxonomy—is a series of six different categories of skills, which ascend from the most basic types to the most complex ones.

 You can learn more about Bloom's Taxonomy in the *A Model of Learning Objectives* section on Iowa State University's Center for Excellence in Learning and Teaching page. You may enjoy the mouse-over interactive graphics that display sample learning outcomes that correspond to key action/outcome verbs. For more information, visit `http://www.celt.iastate.edu/teaching/RevisedBlooms1.html`.

Revised in 2001, there are six levels of Bloom's Taxonomy, which ascend from the lowest to the highest cognitive skills as follows:

- Knowledge/remembering
- Comprehension/understanding
- Application/applying
- Analysis/analyzing
- Evaluation/evaluating
- Synthesis/creating

You can use Bloom's Taxonomy to create your learning outcomes using verbs that describe student learning. Bloom's Taxonomy can help you take a building block approach to teaching and learning by starting with the least complex cognitive skill category (Knowledge/remembering) and then moving up through the levels so that by the end of the course, your students are able to synthesize and create the information.

After you have created the six or seven learning outcomes for your course, keep in mind that you're aiming for outcomes at a variety of different levels. Then, you will need to assemble them in ascending order of complexity. Doing so will help you organize the way you present the material and select your resources and activities. It will also create scaffolding in which your students use the material they've just learned to ascend to the next level.

Universal Design for Learning

Before we start to expand the course, we recommend that you take a moment to plan your course so that it complies with standards and recommendations that have been set to accommodate students' diverse needs and abilities. To do so, we will follow what is referred to as the **Universal Design for Learning** (UDL), which are guidelines that assure accessibility services for individuals with disabilities.

In this section, we will look at legal requirements but keep in mind that the Universal Design for Learning has its roots in ethics, human dignity, and the belief that all individuals deserve to have access to education.

However, in returning to legal frameworks that assure accessibility services to individuals who may have disability issues, let's remember that we must comply with the laws and regulations that have been enacted to provide equal access to them. In the United States, the **Americans with Disabilities Act (ADA)** (1990) protects the civil rights of individuals living with disabilities and requires academic organizations to make educational programs available to students with disabilities. Do not forget to check for similar laws and regulations in your region since they vary from country to country.

We know that each student has a unique set of abilities and strengths and we also realize that all students possess their own learning styles. So, we need to make sure to design courses that are compliant in the following ways and follow the guidelines set forth in the **Higher Education Opportunity Act** of 2008; they follow three primary principles as listed:

- Multiple means of representation
- Multiple means of access and expression
- Multiple means of engagement

In an online course, and a learning management system such as Moodle, you have the flexibility to comply with the previous three principles. For a complete guide to the Higher Education Opportunity Act of 2008, you may visit the U. S. Department of Education website at `http://www2.ed.gov/policy/highered/leg/hea08/index.html`.

Depending on where they live, students with disabilities or special needs may qualify for government-funded programs that provide them with financial support or low-cost assistive technology.

At this point, you may be feeling very nervous and overwhelmed about adhering to complicated rules and regulations. Don't worry; assistive technology has made great strides in the last few years, and many such technologies are very low cost and easy to implement. For example, there are many text-to-voice screen readers and voice recognition programs that convert the spoken word to text. Grand Canyon University has put together an excellent list, which you may find at `http://www.gcu.edu/ Disability-Office/Assistive-Technology.php`.

Don't forget that reasonable accommodation can be achieved in many different ways, ranging from assistive technologies to something as simple as finding a person who can read to a vision impaired learner.

The most important consideration when you're planning your course is preparation. Prepare for students with diverse abilities and needs and design a course that builds in the *multiple means* concept in the Higher Education Opportunity Act of 2008. Remember that it's much more difficult to redesign and retrofit your course than to design it well from the very beginning.

Multiple means of representation

As you plan your course and select course material, remember that you should provide a choice of materials that allow students to achieve the learning outcome. What this means in practical terms is that if you are providing text, you will need to ensure to provide it in a form that can be read by a screen reader for vision impaired learners. If you are providing videos, you will need to include a script for hearing impaired readers. A simple way to achieve this principle is by building in redundancy.

Multiple means of access and expression

As you build your course, be sure to provide different ways for students to act and interact. For example, instead of simply providing readings and quizzes, you may wish to include a discussion forum where you ask your students to discuss questions that help them learn the material and to share drafts of their papers.

You may also want to build in activities that allow students to express themselves by creating documents that include graphics as well as text. In a different case, if you have a student who has difficulty typing, you may allow him/her to turn in an audio recording.

Multiple means of engagement

Student engagement means that students are interacting in the course. They may be interacting with automated quizzes or be engaged in a discussion with their peers. They may also be asked to go online and conduct research.

Moodle has built in many activities that encourage students to use different ways in which to engage with the material in a course. In addition to the forum and a wide array of activities, Moodle also integrates with web conferencing software programs and services, such as BigBlueButton, and offers integration with Skype.

Selecting resources and activities

Now that you can write effective learning outcomes and have used them to build your course framework, which is structured around topics, you are ready to start adding resources and activities.

Keep in mind that each of your topics will contain the following items:

- A summary of your topic as it relates to the course as a whole and the specific content within that topic
- A discussion forum where your students will interact with each other and you as they explain, discuss, and debate subjects that relate to the learning outcomes
- Resources, such as readings, audio lectures, videos, maps, and more, that comprise the course content
- Activities that provide an opportunity to rehearse the skills, reinforce knowledge, and practice the abilities needed for the assessments.

When you add each element, make sure that it directly connects to your learning outcome and you explain how those connections are made. Also, this is a good time to remind yourself of the Universal Design for Learning and how best to meet the needs of students with a wide range of skills and abilities.

Types of assessment

Moodle provides a wide array of options as you determine the best way to let your students demonstrate that they have achieved the knowledge, skills, and abilities that the learning outcomes have defined.

If you've kept in mind the key questions "What do I want my students to *do*?" and "How will they show their skills, knowledge, attitudes, and abilities"?, you will find that it will be much easier to develop the appropriate assessment strategy. The following are a few guidelines:

- Make sure that each topic's assessment ties directly to the learning outcome for that particular topic. Your assessment should be of sufficient complexity to allow your students to demonstrate that they have achieved the learning outcome.

- Each of your resources and activities needs to connect both to the learning outcomes as well as the assessment.

- You should give students an opportunity to practice the assessment and they should be able to obtain feedback when they make errors or need guidance.

- If you have an "end of course" final assessment, make sure that it covers all of the learning outcomes covered in the course.

After you have developed your assessment strategies, you can begin to add them to each of the topics. Make sure that your assessments are clear and straightforward and that they help your students develop a sense of confidence, which will, in turn, encourage them to stay engaged and complete the course.

Some of the ways in which you can help develop self-efficacy and an "I can do it!" attitude that also relate to the overall assessment strategy are as follows:

- Include activities (quizzes, "test your knowledge" multiple-choice questions, and practice tests)

- Include collaborative activities that include peer reviews

- Include interactive graphics

- Use badges and certificates within Moodle to encourage the achievement of mini milestones

Selecting activities that prepare students to perform well in their assessments is a powerful way to achieve learning outcomes and to assure course completion.

Summary

In this chapter, we've learned the best way to write learning outcomes for your course and use them to shape the structure of your course and select resources, activities, and assessments. We explained how and why following the Universal Design for Learning enables students with disabilities to take and succeed in the courses while also complying with legally mandated regulations. We have also reviewed how those learning outcomes (and objectives) affect the selection of resources and activities in your course. In addition, we have described how the type of assessment you use in your course will help demonstrate the student's mastery/ achievement in the course.

In the next chapter, we will guide you through organizing your course. We'll take a close look at how best to match the organization of your course with the overall purpose of the course and the kinds of students you're likely to be teaching.

3
Organizing Your Course

Now that you've determined what you'd like your students to be able to do after they have completed your course and as you're done with the initial planning stages, you are now ready to start building the framework for your course.

Selecting the initial course settings and format allows you to organize your course. In this chapter, we'll learn how to build a structure that accommodates your course content, activities, resources, information, and assessments. In *Chapter 2, Planning Your Course*, you learned how to plan your course with learning outcomes in mind. Now, as we start adding content, thinking about how students will demonstrate their knowledge, skills, and attitudes will help us effectively organize the course. We'll start by building a framework.

As we start to develop the framework, we will include some of the most commonly used elements in Moodle courses. Keep in mind, however, that we're not including everything. Instead, we're aiming to build a basic framework in a step-by-step manner so that by the end of this chapter, you will be in a position to add the content and activities in your course in a clear, coherent way, all the while keeping the overall learning outcomes in mind.

In this chapter, we'll discuss the following topics in terms of organizing your course:

- Course goals
- Course settings
- Course format
- Customizing the appearance of your course

A great way to start thinking about the best structure for your course is by reflecting upon what you want your students to be able to do by the end of the course and the course material that you'll need to include for them to demonstrate that they've achieved the learning outcomes. Keep in mind that it's best to keep your list simple and focused on the essential items rather than on all the potential supplemental or optional material, which might enrich your list but isn't vital.

At this point, you may feel a bit overwhelmed as you review your list and wonder, "what am I going to do with all this material?"

Moodle makes your decisions fun and intuitive because it comes with a number of options that will help you both organize and design your course at the same time.

Our goal is to create a course framework that we can use as a template with which to create functionally consistent courses for use in college degree programs, certificate courses, corporate training, and so on, and what we are doing in this chapter represents a very important step towards achieving it. So, if we keep the big picture in mind and consider the needs and ultimate objectives of the stakeholders, from the learning organization administrators to the curriculum developers, instructional designers, professors/teachers, and students, we will be in a better position to make good decisions as we select the settings and options in Moodle; this will help us make sure that our course is well designed and functional, resulting in a positive learning experience.

Looking at your course goals and the big picture

Let's start by keeping the big picture in mind, not just in terms of learning outcomes and course content, but also in terms of your students and teachers. After all, while you build your course, you may also be developing a demo course or a template that could be used across an entire curriculum and with a broad array of users.

Since both teachers and students have a very diverse range of skills, abilities, and attitudes, it is important to keep their needs in mind as we begin to organize the course and follow the principles of Universal Design for Learning.

Then, as you start creating the structure, consider what your course's home page will look like when students and teachers log in. Keep in mind that many students will use more than one device to access your course and the screens will vary in terms of their size and what they can display.

The following are a few tips for making sure your course structure works well in today's environment of laptops, tablets, smartphones, and desktops, all with varying display sizes:

- Make sure the most important links and information are on the course's home page and that they are visible on the screen of any device

- Test the appearance of your course website on the devices your students and instructors will be using

- Make sure the navigation through your course is simple and consistent and that you use concise, descriptive text for links, and not just "**click here**" or "**click on this link**".

Having a clear, clean course home page will help your students develop confidence as they navigate the course. They will know where to find the materials they need and when and how to access them. In addition, make sure that the links on the course's home page take them directly to the materials they need. This way, your students don't have to click multiple times on multiple drill downs, and they will not feel lost and confused.

 You can learn more about Universal Design for Learning by working through a tutorial made available by the National Center on Low-Incidence Disabilities at the University of Northern Colorado at http://www.unco.edu/cetl/udl/index.html.

As you consider how the organization of your course will help your students perform, and do what they need to do, you can also begin to envision how they will interact with the learning materials and assessments.

Course settings

We created a new course in *Chapter 1, Preparing to Build an Exemplary Moodle Course*, and now we will begin to build the course. Most of the initial course setup will be done through the course settings screen, which you may access through the **Course administration** menu. Remember that when you make changes in the **Course administration** menu, your changes affect only the course you're developing. In our case, it might be a demo course or a template. Remember that changes in the **Site administration** menu or menu are sitewide and apply to all your courses.

As you begin configuring settings, it is a good idea to take a moment to remember the goal to be clear and concise as you select names, create links, and develop content.

The following course settings appear after clicking on **Edit settings** in the **Course administration** menu: **General**, **Description**, **Course format**, **Appearance**, **Files and uploads**, **Completion tracking**, **Guest access**, **Groups**, and **Role renaming**. The **Edit course settings** page is shown in the following screenshot:

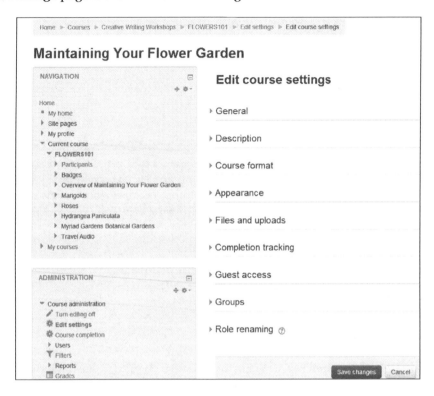

We will work through the basic menu items in the course settings that allow you to set up your course structure and organize your course. For additional information, remember that you can always visit the Moodle Docs at `http://docs.moodle.org/26/en/Main_page`.

General

The first expandable menu, **General**, gives you an opportunity to provide basic information about your course. Please keep in mind that at any time along the way, you may return to the course settings and edit the information.

While it is easy to edit your settings later, it's always best to plan well so that your course descriptions and listings are not ambiguous. The following steps will help you configure the **General** settings:

1. In the **Course administration** menu, click on **Edit settings**. The **Edit course settings** screen will appear.
2. If the **General settings** section is collapsed, click on the menu titled **General to** expand it.
3. Enter data in the following fields: **Course full name**, **Course short name**, **Course category**, **Course start date**, and **Course ID number**.
4. Click on the **Save changes** button.

If your school or organization has a large number of courses, make sure that your course names (including the short names for your courses), the course IDs, and descriptions are consistent with your official course catalog. You will save yourself a great deal of time and frustration if you make sure that everything is consistent at the outset, rather than trying to retrofit or correct it later. Aim for clear, concise language and terminology that is consistent across your organization and its course catalog.

Description

Although you may have a lengthy course description in the course catalog along with additional text that describes the course outcomes, you may not want to include it all in the description.

Instead, in the **Course summary** box, type a brief description that captures the essence of your course. Note that the box includes a number of web-editing tools that allow you to customize the appearance of the description. This capability will be very helpful later when we look at the overall appearance of the course page.

You may also use the **Course summary files** box that gives you the opportunity to upload files using the **Add** option or drag-and-drop them. Using **Course summary files** gives you an opportunity to incorporate multiple modalities in adherence to the principles of Universal Design for Learning so that your course information is in text as well as audio and/or video format. By making your course information available in audio and video format, you will be making your material accessible to a wide array of learners.

For example, you may insert the link to an audio file (MP3 is ideal) or a video you have uploaded on YouTube or insert the link to an embedded player. You may also include a link to an expanded text file that includes more detailed information.

Course format

Below the **Description** section, you will see **Course format**. As you expand it, you'll see several options, which have expandable menus.

Structuring your instructional material using a format

A format allows you to develop the structure of your instructional material. This is a critical decision, and you must make it carefully. If at all possible, your format should be consistent across your curriculum so that all your courses have a similar look, feel, and organization.

Notice there are a number of options that automatically generate a preformatted set of fields, which makes it easy for you to enter data. The various formats available are as follows:

- The **Topics format**
- The **Weekly format**
- The **Social format**
- The **Single activity format**

Most schools, colleges, universities, and organizations will use either the **Topics** or the **Weekly** formats. For example, if your college follows a 16-week semester format, it is often useful to follow a weekly format.

However, many colleges and universities offer the same courses over varying spans of time and may offer a 4-week, 8-week, 12-week, or 16-week term. In such cases, it is often helpful to select the **Topics format** and then specify the timeline by means of a link to a calendar that includes the due dates for the course term.

The number of sections of the course

The number of sections in a course corresponds to the *functional chunks* of the instructional material and activities that the students will work through in the course. Each organization will have its own approach to delivering coursework, with terms that may vary.

If your organization offers 4-week, 8-week, and 16-week options, it is a good idea to divide your content and activities into sections that can be either expanded or compressed. For example, you may select eight topics, and if you are in a position where your school offers the course in 4-week, 8-week, and 16-week terms, you may easily double up and accelerate through the course's content at twice the regular pace, or simply spread the content out over two weeks instead of one.

On the other hand, if your organization wants to offer everything in a single week, or the course is very brief and intended to be completed in several hours, you may wish to break the content into sections that correspond to the amount of time that will be spent on the task.

Keep the following points in mind:

- Make your sections consistent in terms of the amount of content each contains
- Try to keep the amount of time needed to complete each task consistent

Hidden sections

Hidden sections allow you to avoid distracting your students with too much information on the screen. There may be a few situations where you may wish to make all sections visible. Such cases may occur in a very brief course that requires the students to have all the information while working through the course.

Course layout

You may either show all the sections on one page, or choose to show one section per page. If your course only contains two sections, you may wish to show them on a single page.

However, in the interest of clarity, it is often a good idea to show one section per page. Again, be sure to think ahead and consider what you'd like your students to be doing as they navigate through the course and what they should be able to do by the end of the course. Make sure that the structure of your course guides them along a clear path. Keep in mind that the course introduction topic will be visible on each page, even when you have one topic per page.

Appearance

The **Appearance** menu, shown in the following screenshot, allows you to create a universal look and feel for your entire course:

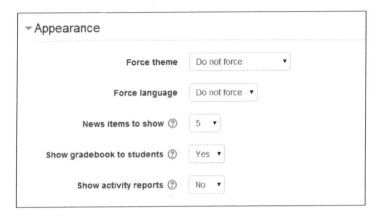

The options are self-explanatory, but there are a few key points to keep in mind as you organize your course:

- **Force theme**: This option allows you to apply a specific theme across the entire course, rather than giving your students an opportunity to modify it if the option is selected. If you choose **Do not force**, the theme that you have selected site wide will be used.

- **News items to show**: This option gives you a chance to create announcements in a special box on the course page. Include this if you have important announcements, key dates, and reminders for your course. Avoid including too many items, because they can be distracting and also chew up valuable digital real estate on your course page.

- **Show gradebook to students**: This option helps you to allow your students to check their grades, which can be extremely motivating and a key to their success.

- **Show activity reports**: This option permits students to see their own activity reports, which can be quite helpful.

Files and uploads

You may select the upper limit of files and uploads. The upper limit can be set by the Moodle administrator in accordance with the needs of those using the site. Our recommendation is to set the limit to 10 MB and to use best practices in web design such as file compression to keep file sizes to a minimum. For larger files, we recommend using repositories that integrate with Moodle such as YouTube, Dropbox, and Equella. For example, instead of uploading large files, such as videos, it's much better to use an HTML5 friendly video player, which you may embed. If your students are creating large files as part of their coursework, you may encourage them to upload those files to SoundCloud (if they're audio files), YouTube (if they're video files), and SlideShare (if they're PowerPoint presentations, and especially if they contain large graphics).

For maximum accessibility and to comply with Universal Design for Learning, keep in mind that HTML works very well with assistive technologies that convert text to voice for individuals with impaired vision. If possible, convert your presentations and documents to a format that can be used by assistive technology.

For individuals with impaired hearing and/or cognitive disabilities, providing a written script to accompany audio files can help you achieve the goal of using multiple modalities for optimizing student accessibility to the course content.

For student papers or projects, a maximum upload size of 2 MB is often sufficient, especially if they use ZIP files.

Completion tracking

Along with the **Show gradebook to students** option, the **Completion tracking** option can help students maintain their levels of motivation and develop a positive, "I can do it!" approach, which translates to self-efficacy and self-determination.

By being able to track when they complete their units and/or activities, students can stay motivated and continue to set and meet their personal goals.

Guest access

You may wish to allow members of your instructional design team, instructional technologists, or other observers to have access to your course. If this is the case, make sure that you set **Allow guest access** to **Yes**.

Groups

Moodle allows you to set up student groups while you are developing the framework of the course. It is often a good idea to set up groups, even if you have collaborative activities, or you'd like to give individuals a chance to work and share in informal teams. Groups can also be very effective for peer reviews of papers or projects.

However, if your course does not include collaborative/team activities or peer reviews, setting up groups can add an unnecessary level of complexity to your course.

Role renaming

Moodle's default names for roles within the course are very straightforward and intuitive, especially the roles **Manager**, **Teacher**, and **Student**.

However, you may wish to rename the roles to correspond with the role names used in your organization. For example, a corporation may prefer the word `Facilitator` instead of **Teacher** and a **Student** may be termed `Team Member` or `Learner`.

 A cautionary note is in order here. If your organization has a number of courses, it is a good idea to make sure that the roles have consistent names and that you do not rename roles in every course. Maintaining consistency will help you avoid confusion and frustration.

After you have completed all the tasks in **Edit course settings**, click on the **Save changes** button.

Customizing your course page

Let's return to your course's home page, which is not the same as your front page or portal. Instead, we're focusing on developing the course itself.

Are there a few items that we need to include that we were not able to customize when we edited the course page? This section discusses a few items you may wish to include.

The Calendar block

Including a calendar which demarcates course events can help your students stay on track. To add a calendar, you will first add a **Calendar** block as shown in the following steps:

1. Click on the **Turn editing on** button.
2. In the **Add a block** menu, click on **Add...**.
3. Click on **Calendar** in the drop-down menu. A **Calendar** block will appear on the course page.
4. Click on the Actions icon in the **Calendar** block and select **Configure Calendar block** to configure the options you wish to have displayed.
5. Click on the **Save changes** button.

To add events, just click on the month of the event in the **Calendar** block, and then click on **New event**. The new event can apply to the course, the user, or the website.

If you use a calendar, you may wish to include the following items: course start date, course end date, key due dates, and also any administrative issues that could be of value. You can add each of these items in the individual course calendars for courses.

Instructor/institution links

Instead of incorporating a large graphic of your institution along with the institution's mission and vision statement, you may wish to use an HTML block to include a quick link to the institution's web page; this is most useful for your purposes.

You may also wish to include a link to the instructor's contact information, if it is an instructor-led course.

Student success links

To keep your website very neat, it is often useful to gather all student support sites in a single place. So, you may wish to create a **Page** resource or, if the list is short, another HTML block that includes resources such as links to the Help desk, the Online Library, the Writing Center, and other support areas.

Additional elements to customize the appearance of your course

We've discussed the general appearance of your course, but there are a few additional items that will allow you to customize the appearance of your course. As you make changes, you may wish to keep accessibility in mind and use the guidelines of Universal Design for Learning.

Fonts

Moodle gives you many options for design, and you may notice that web-editing boxes pop up almost every time you add content. While it's very tempting to use a wide array of colors, fonts, and symbols, be sure to keep it simple. The following are a few key points:

- Choose fonts carefully and use them consistently.
- Use a Sans Serif font, such as Arial or Helvetica. They are easier for people with impaired vision to read. They will be displayed uniformly in most browsers.
- If you are using graphics with text, be aware that magnification software often results in highly pixelated text and can be hard to read.
- If you code in HTML, use relative sizes rather than absolute sizes for the font. If you use absolute sizes, you essentially "lock down" the sizing and it is not possible for magnification software to enlarge it then.
- Avoid using too many colors.

Images

Images can be a very powerful way to add personality and individual branding to your courses. However, it's also easy to add too many images or to overwhelm the students with large, potentially irrelevant images. For this reason, be sure to keep in mind the following points:

- Use meaningful graphics
- Place them so that they add and reinforce meaning (rather than distract or confuse students)
- Optimize the size of images so that they load quickly
- If you need to use large graphics, create a clickable thumbnail that expands to a large graphic (for example, a map)

Theme considerations

Let's return, for a moment, to **Appearance** in the **Site administration** menu. One of the ways to change the look and feel of your course is using themes. Moodle has a wide array of built-in themes that can be utilized to give your course a customized look and feel. It is often worthwhile to use a theme developed by a Moodle developer. Many are free and others can be licensed. Themes can be particularly useful if you are using multiple devices and you want your course to automatically display content well for tablets, laptops, smartphones, desktops, and other handheld devices.

For example, if you would like a theme that is optimized for multiple devices and works equally well with laptops, tablets, and smartphones, you may wish to select the **Simple** theme. It is flexible for individuals with impaired vision, and the font sizes and column heights can be adjusted by the users. An example of how the **Simple** theme works on multiple devices is shown in the following figure:

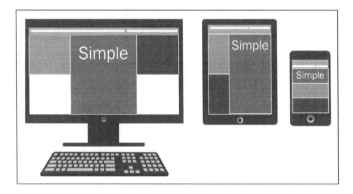

If you would like a clean, crisp look for your course that enables you to easily customize it to get a recognizable, unique brand, you may wish to select the fluid-width, three-column **Contemporary** theme. **Contemporary** is a contributed theme. It is a plugin that has been developed by a third-party vendor and works well with standard Moodle installations. To find more themes, you can visit the Moodle plugins directory at `https://moodle.org/plugins/browse.php?list=category&id=3`.

To install one of these contributed themes, see the Moodle Docs page for installing add-ons at http://docs.moodle.org/26/en/Installing_add-ons. Once installed, a theme can be selected by going to **Site administration** | **Appearance** | **Themes**, and then click on **Theme selector**. You'll have an opportunity to click on the button **Change theme** and select from the options. After you select the **Clean** theme from the available options, you will see the selected theme in the **Theme selector** settings, as shown in the following screenshot:

Summary

In this chapter, we explored how to organize your course in terms of its structure, format, and appearance. We learned the best way to use Moodle's built-in course settings and elements to create a framework that can be consistent and flexible for all your courses. For example, you can develop a demo course and use it as a template or guide for future courses. We discussed the reasons for making certain decisions as we develop the framework and how to think about the best ways to make your course accessible for all your students.

In the next chapter, we will guide you through developing content and activities for your course. We'll take a close look at how best to match your course materials with the overall purpose of the course and how to do so in a way that is motivating and engaging to students and encourages students' success.

4
Best Practices in Content Delivery

In *Chapter 3, Organizing Your Course*, we learned how to develop different types of structures for your courses and how to customize them so that they meet the needs of your institution, students, and instructors.

Now we are ready to look at the content of the course, which will include the course material as well as activities and assessments. We will look at the best ways to deliver your content, which involves reviewing the types of content, formats, and tools.

If you take a look at your Moodle installation, you may feel overwhelmed at the number of choices that you have.

We're going to streamline the approach by looking at three different categories of content: resources, activities, and assessments. Considering this approach, it will be much easier for us to cover all that we need to, in order to create a course that helps us achieve our desired learning outcomes as well as accommodate all kinds of learners.

In this chapter, we'll show you the best ways to deliver content in your Moodle course, which includes:

- Managing types of content
- Adding resources
- Adding key activities
- Incorporating assessments
- Using tools to build more complex content

Managing types of content

Your Moodle course may be fairly simple with basic instructional materials, assessments, and tools for interaction. Even at its most basic, though, you'll have to be mindful of the following few key points:

- To accommodate diverse learning styles and devices, it is best to offer your content in different formats, which includes a combination of presentations, text, audio, graphics, videos, and forums/messaging

- To engage students and to give them chances to demonstrate their knowledge and skills, include a range of activities such as assignments and discussion forums

- To assess what students are learning, offer a variety of assessments such as quizzes

- To reduce filesystem overload on the on-premises server, you may wish to use cloud-based sites, such as YouTube, SlideShare, and so on, rather than uploading large files to the Moodle server

As we get started, let's keep in mind that for convenience, we're trying to start with a simple, straightforward approach. We can always increase the complexity as we go forward.

Adding resources to our course

Resources make it possible for all the students to have access to the same course material. It's also possible for you to organize the content in a way that ties well with your course objectives, which then connect to activities and assessments.

There are a number of resources to choose from; however, we will focus on the ones you're most likely to use in your course. To add a resource, follow the steps found for each resource.

Adding course materials via Book

The **Book** resource allows you to assemble multiple pages in a single location, and to organize them with an automatically generated table of contents. The book resource is mobile friendly and easy to print. It works very well with flowable themes. It's convenient, particularly if you're using it for the course syllabus or an e-book text. The downside is that you're customizing your content for a single location within your Moodle course, which makes it complicated if you're planning to use the same text for multiple courses. In that case, it's better to house your content in a single location outside Moodle and then link it in Moodle.

The following are the steps to add the **Book** resource:

1. In the **Course administration** menu, click on **Turn editing on**.

2. Go to the topic where you'd like to add content. and click on **Add an activity or resource**.

3. Review the menu of resources.

4. Click on the resource you want to add, such as **Book**.

5. Fill in the fields on the screen **Adding a new Book**, and click on **Save and display**.

6. Fill in the fields on your book screen and click on **Save changes**.

You may view the **Adding a new Book** page in the following screenshot:

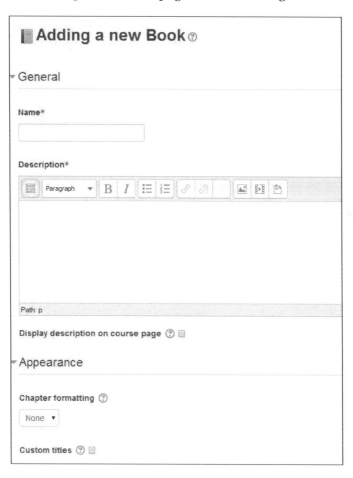

Adding files

One of the easiest ways to ensure that your students are able to obtain the same content is to upload the course material via separate files. Clustering files together will allow your students to find the material for your course easily. Typical files include text files along with graphics, audio files, videos, and presentations. Keep in mind that not everyone will have the same software. We recommend that you convert your content into a PDF format so that you can upload a PDF file rather than a PowerPoint file or a text file. This will ensure that the formatting and fonts stay the same for your intellectual property to be more easily preserved, because it is harder to copy graphics from a PDF file than from a PowerPoint file. If you convert the files to PDF, your students can open them if they have installed the free Adobe Acrobat Reader. The advantage is that the formatting and fonts will not change (as your students might have different versions of presentation and word-processing software).

Adding folders

If you have a number of files that fall into a single category or topic, you may wish to group them together in a folder. The folder resource allows you to present many files in one place through one link on the course page.

The main advantage of the folder is that it allows you to avoid a cluttered page, or one that requires too much scrolling.

The disadvantage of using folders is that you may require too many clicks; content can be invisible or deeply buried, and thus easy for students to overlook or miss.

 Use subfolders to organize the files you want to provide, but don't overdo it because they can be deeply buried and no one will notice them.

Adding pages

With the **Page** resource, you're able to use the built-in web editor to create a simple website that can contain links, graphics, and embedded HTML codes. You can use an embedded HTML code and make it very easy for students to access cloud-based resources, such as videos on YouTube.com, audios on SoundCloud.com, presentations on SlideShare.com, photos and graphics on Flickr.com, and so on.

Since the embedded HTML code often contains players, it's possible to stream the media rather than having to wait for the files to download. The advantages of this include ease of access and saving of time. The disadvantage is that you must be connected to the Internet to stream the video files. You may prefer to download the files to your device in order to play them when you're not connected to the Internet.

Embedding presentations

You can use embedded HTML code for presentations as well. This is important for two reasons. First, you may wish to avoid bandwidth and problems caused due to slow download, by hosting in the cloud. So, in that case, using services such as SlideShare.com can be a lifesaver. Second, you may wish to protect intellectual property by not making it too easy to copy sensitive (and popular) graphics, charts, maps, and so on. In that case, you can protect yourself by making the presentation available in the PDF format rather than PowerPoint or another easily copied and dissected format. It does not prevent your ideas from being stolen , but at least it slows down people with ill intent and makes it more difficult for them to copy and paste.

For another layer of safety, you can record yourself giving your presentation on BigBlueButton.org (a webinar program that is open source with free downloads for Moodle installations after Moodle 2.5). Or, alternatively, you can make a movie using a screen recording program such as Camtasia. Then, you can upload your presentation to YouTube.com or Flickr.com, where it will be very difficult for anyone to copy your intellectually unique graphics.

Adding activities

The main difference between a Moodle resource and a Moodle activity is that a resource tends to be static while an activity involves student performance. Activities are used for communication, collaboration, practice, performance, and assessment.

The following are the steps to add activities:

1. In the **Course administration** menu, click on **Turn editing on**.
2. Go to the topic where you'd like to add content and click on **Add an activity or resource**.
3. View the menu of activities.
4. Click on the activity you want to add.

 You can learn more about activities and activity settings at http://docs.moodle.org/26/en/Activities.

Assignment module

The **Assignment** module creates a structure that makes it convenient for both students and instructors to assign and turn in work, then grade it and provide feedback.

You can set the **Assignment** module for students to perform a task, and then upload a file that you will then grade. The **Assignment** module is an activity, and it can also be considered an assessment because you're able to set grades and criteria, and you can specify the type of submissions that you'll accept. You can also set the grading criteria by clicking on the **Grade** link and specifying the number of points, the grade scale and method of grading, the grade category, and marking allocation. The number of points, the grade scale (these are the same things), and the grade category can be set either through gradebook or through the **Assignment** settings; the method of grading (simple or advanced) can be set through the **Grading method** drop-down menu.

Choice

The **Choice** activity is a multiple choice poll that can be used to engage students at any point during a course. It can be used as an engager, for example, in a "Did You Know?" or "Test Your Knowledge" type of single-question poll. It can also be used to quickly review facts.

Forum

A **forum** is a powerful tool for communication and collaboration. It's also a great place to deliver content, because you can upload files or provide links to content within the different threads in the **Forum** activity. The advantage of delivering content through a forum is that it's easy to ask students to respond to specific questions about the content and to keep the students focused. The downside is that it's fairly labor intensive to use the **Forum** activity to distribute content, especially if you require the same content to go in a number of different courses. In that case, it's easier to add it in a **Page** resource.

Lesson

A **lesson** provides both content and interaction. You can include files, links, and custom pages. The basic structure of a lesson is a series of HTML pages. You can include multiple choice questions, short answer questions, true/false questions, matching and essay type questions; when the students select an answer, they are directed to another page. Through planning, you can create adaptive lessons, which take students on a path that is individualized according to their choices. The downside of the lesson is that it requires quite a bit of time to be set up and can be quite complex. The following screenshot is the setup screen for a lesson in a topic entitled **Social Media**:

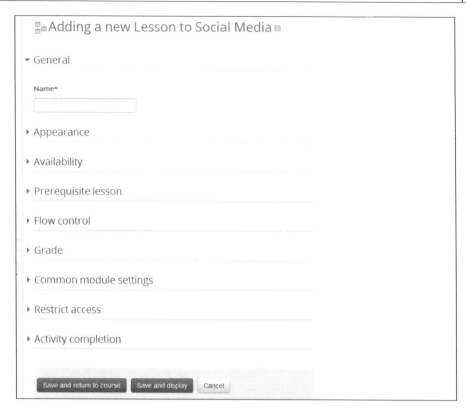

Here is a simplified approach that simply focuses on a lesson, which requires students to turn in an essay. So, instead of multiple-choice questions, it simply allows students to access materials, turn in an essay, and then receive feedback from the instructor.

1. Go to your course and click on **Turn editing on**. Select **Lesson** from the **Add an activity or resource** link.

2. Fill in the fields in the drop-down menus where you'd like to add content.

3. Go to your lesson and add content, and then click on **Save and display**. You'll have the following options listed; however, in reality, it's easier to add a content page, and then add a question page. If you do so, you'll have a very straightforward lesson with questions and a graded essay that students will turn in.

   ○ **Import questions**
   ○ **Add a content page**
   ○ **Add a cluster**
   ○ **Add a question page**

4. You may edit your instructions and provide guidance by clicking on **Add a content** page, which you'll include before or after the question page.

One of the advantages of using **Lesson** is that it allows you to put the instructions, the lesson readings and materials, the questions, grading, and grade reports together in a single location. This is very convenient for students and instructors. The following screenshot shows the preview of your lesson:

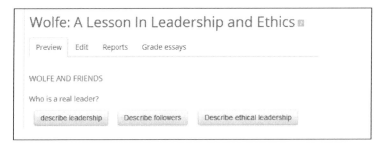

The following screenshot shows the **Edit** tab on a lesson's page:

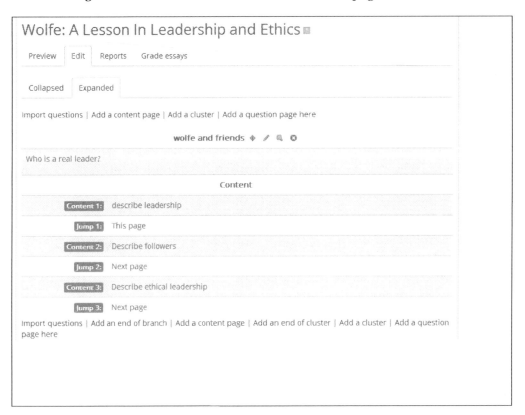

As you can see, at any point, you can modify the content in a number of different ways to make your lesson very robust, yet simple to follow, since the components are contained in a single place. So, students can go to a single location to take a quiz or survey, add readings, videos, graphics, and more.

Quiz

The **Quiz** activity module includes a number of options, which include self-scoring questions, and ones that include feedback and the correct responses for each response so that the student has a chance to review the material. The **Quiz** module allows you to choose the types of questions from a list of options such as:

- **Calculated**
- **Calculated multichoice**
- **Calculated simple**
- **Embedded answers (Cloze)**
- **Essay**
- **Matching**
- **Multiple choice**
- **Numerical**
- **Short answer**
- **True/False**
- **Description**

After you have selected the type of questions, you will begin to develop a data bank. You'll fill in the question form, and assign grades for the correct answer.

Once you've created a question, you'll add the response and feedback. Each time you add a question, you'll also be adding it to your Question Bank. Be sure to include the question and also the response/feedback.

The **Quiz** activity module is a very convenient and flexible way to help students assess their knowledge. It's also a great way to deliver content (feedback and review) in a way that engages students.

The disadvantage is that a **Quiz** activity can take quite a bit of time to set up. Generally, it's not easy to create questions and responses that are psychometrically sound.

Wiki

The **Wiki** activity gives you the chance to deliver content and build it at the same time. In Moodle, **Wiki** is often used when it's considered desirable for class members to contribute to a single project, which would be a set of web pages on a certain topic or set of topics. The **Wiki** activity can be a collection of information on a topic or examples, or it could be a report on a single topic which contains enough complexity to allow individual students to contribute, review, and edit a section or part of an entry.

The advantage of a wiki is that it's collaborative and easy to use. The disadvantage is that it can become chaotic and muddled, and one or two individuals can dominate.

Using assessments to deliver content

Assessments are not, strictly speaking, course content, but it is possible to deliver course content in a quiz or assignment. However, some assessments can be good places to deliver content, particularly if the course requires content of maps, parts, or procedures.

For example, a quiz built on matching content could involve matching illustrations to a label or a concept. In that case, the content being delivered would be the diagram or graphic material.

Backing up and reusing activities

Once you've built content and a delivery system, it's a good idea to reuse the course or parts of the course. You can reuse activities in a number of ways. Moodle offers you the ability to reuse your course, or part of the course within the same Moodle system or another Moodle, by using the Backup/Restore function.

The following are the steps to reuse activities and parts of activities:

1. In the **ADMINISTRATION** block, click on **Assignment administration**.
2. From the options, select **Backup**.
3. Check the boxes next to the types of items to backup.
4. Click on **Next** on the screen and rename the file if desired.
5. Download the file and save it to a location where you can retrieve it easily at a later date.

To back up a single activity from your course, follow the same procedure. If you want to reuse content within the same Moodle site, you may simply restore them. If you want to use them on a different Moodle site, download them and save them locally.

Summary

In this chapter, we reviewed ways to deliver content, either by adding resources or activities. We looked at the most commonly used resources and activities and we discussed when and why they are used. We reviewed their advantages and disadvantages, and explained when to use them effectively in our courses.

Finally, we looked at the connections between content delivery and assessments, and we touched on course management and how to save time by backing up activities so that they can be reused later.

In the next chapter, we will look at specific types of courses, and learn the best ways to build them.

5
Designing Self-paced Independent Study Courses

Being able to take a course at any time, any place, and at your own pace makes online course offerings very popular. While many courses are instructor led and may involve extensive interaction with other students, there are also many courses that are self guided and contain self-scoring and adaptive assessments that do not require interaction with an instructor or other students.

With Moodle, you can create standalone, self-paced, and independent study courses that can be used in many settings and for various purposes. They may be short training courses that all employees must take for safety, health, or regulatory compliance purposes. They could be review courses on certain subjects or courses that are created for a wide audience or just for fun.

In this chapter, you'll learn how to develop a consistent look and feel for all your self-paced independent study courses. We'll review plugins, resources, and activities that you will find useful to include. We'll then learn how to set up the courses at the individual course level and review the best ways to add resources, activities, and assessments. We'll also discuss how to make sure that your students can track their progress and how to automatically generate customized certificates upon course completion. Finally, we'll learn how to set up badges, build them, and also enable social media so your students can display them.

In this chapter, we'll discuss the following topics:

- Configuring global settings for self-paced independent study courses
- Selecting ideal plugins, activities, resources, and assessments
- Tracking progress and checking grades

- Designing customized, automatically generated certificates
- Incorporating badges and other social media
- Creating an effective assessment strategy
- Developing self-paced independent study

Self-paced independent study

Self-paced independent study means that your students are working on their own and that they will not have any direct interaction with an instructor or other students. Thus, there are a number of elements in Moodle that you will not need to include in your course website. For example, you will not need a forum and activities that require grading by an instructor.

At the same time, if students are working on their own, you may need to include self-help elements. You'll definitely need tools, such as a progress tracker, to help students know where they stand in the course, and you'll need to make sure that your instructional material, activities, and assessments tie together very clearly. You can build in activities such as low-stakes self-grading quizzes that keep students engaged and motivated. Keeping students motivated is critical because self-paced classes require students to motivate themselves and there is no teacher or tutor to provide external structure.

 You can learn more about how building in automated feedback can motivate students in the *Five Principles of Successful Course Redesign* article on the National Center for Academic Transformation page at http://www.thencat.org/PlanRes/R2R_PrinCR.htm.

Self-paced independent study courses can vary widely in their length, scope, complexity, and "stakes". Some can be completed in less than an hour, while others may be intended for completion over a semester. They can be offered by colleges, universities, corporations, not-for-profit organizations, retailers, and other organizations that need to provide educational courses and training.

Configuring your course – global settings

The more consistent you can make your courses, the better. There may be a bit of a learning curve the first time a student takes a course, but if the second course has the same look, feel, and functionality, chances are, the student will feel more confident. The students' user experience is very important.

We can make sure that our courses are consistent by configuring the courses in **Site administration**, which will assure us that the settings apply sitewide and are, essentially, global. So, let's get started by looking at the best way to configure the global settings.

Theme selection

If your students are accessing your course using a wide array of devices, including laptops, desktop computers, smartphones, and tablets, you may wish to select a responsive theme that "flows" across devices. A responsive theme will be displayed appropriately across multiple devices.

This section shows you how to get started on developing the ideal look and feel for your independent study course. Fundamental to the course design is the selection of a theme, which may seem odd; however, in this case, selecting the theme is critical for many reasons ranging from the course being displayed across multiple devices to being easy to navigate.

The **Clean** theme, which was new in Moodle 2.5 and is available as a core theme in Moodle 2.6, is highly recommended because it automatically displays across multiple devices and also comprises very little formatting/styling. Let's select the **Clean** theme and configure the settings as follows:

1. From the **ADMINISTRATION** block in the **Site administration** menu, click on **Appearance**.
2. Click on **Themes**.
3. Click on **Theme settings**.
4. On the **Theme settings** screen, click on the default selections for all the menu items. Make sure that the **Default: Yes** checkbox is checked for **Enable device detection**.
5. Click on the **Save changes** button.

For more information on the **Clean** theme, you may visit the blog post on the following website:

```
http://www.somerandomthoughts.com/blog/2013/05/08/moodle-2-5-and-the-
bootstrap-based-theme-clean/
```

Activities

As we configure the courses and set the global settings, let's take a look at the activities in Moodle.

Most activities you will be using will use default settings. However, there are a few that may require customization, such as **Quiz**, **Book**, and **Badge**.

Quiz

Because the default settings may not be appropriate for your organization, you may wish to change some of the options. When you make changes in the **Quiz** activity, the values you set will be the default values used globally. Perform the following steps to configure the **Quiz** plugin:

1. In the **Site administration** menu, click on **Plugins**.
2. Click on **Activities modules**.
3. Click on **Quiz**.
4. On the **Quiz** screen, review the different options. You may wish to update the settings, such as the **Time limit (seconds)** setting, and restrict students to a fixed number of attempts (rather than maintaining the default setting, that is, **Unlimited**),
5. Click on the **Save changes** button.

Review some of the other plugins in the **Site administration** menu. Keep in mind that we may not use all the options. For more information, refer to the Moodle Docs (http://docs.moodle.org/26/en/Main_page) for Moodle 2.6.

Book

The **Book** plugin is a great way to create an online text for your students.

To configure the Book plugin, perform the following steps:

1. In the **Site administration** menu, click on **Plugins**.
2. Click on **Activity modules**.
3. Click on **Book**.
4. On the **Book** screen, set the option for **Chapter formatting**. We recommend **Numbers**.

Badges

Badges, which were new in Moodle 2.5, are very useful for motivating students to complete their courses. When students complete a learning module that involves a skill and a summative assessment, they can begin working on their course assessments. You can set up the course to automatically generate badges when students achieve their goals. Then, they can display the badge in their "backpack" or on social media sites such as Facebook. Mozilla's Open Badges project includes a Badges Backpack in which badges can be displayed.

Let's configure our courses for badges. Remember, we are enabling the badges sitewide. You may also configure and upload badges for individual courses by performing the following steps:

1. In the **Site administration** menu, click on **Badges**.
2. Click on **Badges settings**.
3. On the **Badges settings** screen, type in the name of your organization or the issuing agent. Then, include your e-mail address. Make sure that you check **Yes** for **Enable connection to external backpacks** and **Enable course badges**.
4. Click on **Save changes**.

To add a badge, perform the following steps:

1. In the **Site administration** menu, click on **Badges**.
2. Click on **Manage badges** and then click on the **Add a new badge** button.
3. On the **Badge details** screen, type the name and a description of the badge. Then upload an image. This will be the badge image that will be displayed. It should be in the .jpeg or .gif formats and no larger than 200 x 200 pixels in size.
4. Click on **Create badge**.

 You can learn more about badges in the Mozilla Open Badges project at http://openbadges.org/. You can also sign up for a backpack in which you can display your badges at backpack.openbadges.org.

To create a unique design for your badge, which incorporates your own photos, you can use free web-based photo editing such as PicMonkey (http://www.picmonkey.com/), which is an easy-to-use cloud-based program that does not require registration.

The following image is a rather whimsical example, which took about five minutes to create using PicMonkey:

PicMonkey offers a wide array of elements that allow you to upload and modify your own photos or create your own design using stock elements.

To manage a badge within an individual course, perform the following steps:

1. In the **Course administration** menu, click on **Badges**.

2. Click on **Manage badges**.

3. Click on the name of the badge you want to edit. On the **Badges details** screen, you will see the following tabs: **Overview**, **Edit details**, **Criteria**, **Message**, and **Recipients**. Enter the criteria for issuing the badge in each of the screens.

4. Click on **Save changes**.

Calendar

Assuming that all individuals start a course on a specific date, it might not be a bad idea to create a calendar if the course takes more than a week or so to be completed. For example, you may be offering month-long courses and the students can start working on them at the beginning of every month.

Let's set up a calendar for a course that lasts 30 days using the following steps:

1. Go to the **Site administration** menu.

2. Click on **Appearance**.

3. Click on **Calendar**.

4. Modify **Days to look ahead** to **30** and also change the default settings for **Events to Lookahead**.

5. Click on **Save changes**.

Course-level configuration

Now that you've configured the course at the site level, you will need to configure the elements at the course level and make sure that they are ideal for self-paced independent study. So, go to the **Course administration** menu.

Course settings

Let's take a look at the course settings. We'll want to make sure that the course is arranged in an "any time / any place / any pace" way. The following are the ideal course settings:

1. In the **ADMINISTRATION** block, go to **Course administration**.
2. Click on **Edit settings**.
3. Select the course format as **Topics format** and as you do so, add at least two more topics (in addition to those that will be units in your course). You'll use one of the topics for the instructional material that you'll be using throughout the entire course. The other topic will include practice tests/exams/quizzes.
4. In the **Appearance** section, select **Yes** for **Show gradebook to students**.
5. In the **Completion tracking** section, **Enable completion tracking** should be set to **Yes**.
6. In the **Groups** section, make sure that you do not include groups. So, select **No groups**.
7. Click on Save changes.

Course completion

Course completion is very critical in self-paced courses. The following are the ideal settings:

1. In the **Course administration** menu, click on **Course completion**.
2. In order to use **Course completion**, you must set up your course completely. So, all activities and resources must exist in the course in order for it to be set up. On the **Edit course completion settings** page, open the options. In **General**, select **Course is complete when ALL conditions are met**. In **Condition: Activity completion**, check all the activities that must be completed. Select **ALL selected activities to be completed**.

The following screenshot illustrates **Condition: Activity completion** field:

3. In the other settings, you may choose the default settings or add your own conditions depending on your preferences.

4. Click on **Save changes**.

Resources

Organize your resources around your topics. For resources that students will use in the entire course, create a topic and name it Course materials. Other resources can be added to each topic.

To select a resource, perform the following steps

1. In the **Home** menu, click on your course.

2. Select **Add an activity or resource**.

Book

You've already configured the **Book** resources so that they have a look and feel that is consistent across all your courses. Now, for each individual course, you may add HTML files that you can combine and present as a book. You can even enable students to download them. To configure the **Book** resources, perform the following steps:

1. On your course page, click on **Add an activity or resource**.
2. Select **Book**.
3. On the **Adding a new Book** screen, add the name and description.
4. On the **Editing chapter** screen, enter your content into the **Content** box.
5. Click on **Save changes**.

You can update and change your book and its contents by adding material.

Resources

Let's start with resources. Having understood your subject and defined the learning outcomes of each topic, it's time to gather and organize your resources. For a self-paced course, you may consider using the types of resources described in this section.

In general, to add resources, click on **Add an activity or a resource**. Check the drop-down menu or simply drag-and-drop them in the course area.

Resources – File

Using the **File** resource to add resources is very effective. Make sure that your file is in a format that your students will be able to download. For example, it's a good idea to upload a PDF file rather than a Microsoft Word document.

Presentations (slide shows) can be uploaded as PDFs in order to avoid problems with versions and compatibility when using Keynote or PowerPoint.

Scripts and notes of your presentations can be uploaded as PDF or HTML. HTML is a good choice if you have students with low vision because screen-reader software uses HTML.

Audio files / podcasts can be uploaded directly or hosted with a service such as SoundCloud (or YouTube). Allowing MP3 downloads is often a good idea because students may wish to download the files and play them on their MP3 players or smartphones.

Resources – URL

If file sizes are large, it is often a good idea to first create the presentations / course content and then upload them to a cloud-based hosting service. If you do so, you may need to be able to create your presentations in different formats.

The following sections are guidelines for a number of different types of presentations.

Recording webcasts/presentations

One popular approach to creating a narrated presentation is using screen capture software in which you record audio as you make your presentation. You can then save and upload the presentation to a number of sites, such as YouTube, Flickr, and UStream.tv. The advantages of using screen capture software are that the quality tends to be high, and there is quite a bit of flexibility. The disadvantages are that there can be a steep learning curve and the software licenses can be expensive.

For high-quality audio, be sure to invest in a good headset microphone. Avoid using the built-in microphone on your computer. When you record using your headset, be sure to double check the settings to make sure that they not default to the built-in microphone.

CamStudio (`http://www.camstudio.org`) is a free open source program that records screen motion and audio and saves them as AVI files. It then converts them to SWF (flash). There are obvious limitations with this software program (that is, the Flash files will not play on all devices and platforms).

QuickTime (built-in on Mac) has built-in screen recording that can record the entire screen or part of it, with or without audio or audio only.

The following are a few free (some have limited functionality) products for screencasts. We're only including the ones that include audio, as follows:

- **ActivePresenter**: For this product, please visit `http://atomisystems.com/activepresenter/free-edition/`.

  This product can save screencasts in numerous formats.

- **BB FlashBack Express**: For this product, please visit `http://www.bbsoftware.co.uk/`.

  This product can save screencasts as flash or AVI that can be "one-click" uploads to YouTube.

- **Jing**: For this product, please visit `http://www.techsmith.com/jing.html`.

  You can't include audio, but Jing is a very easy and convenient way to create screen captures and videos, and then upload them. Jing works for both Mac and Windows operating systems.

- For this product, please visit `http://www.screenpresso.com/featuresall`.

  This product is portable, that is, you do not have to download it. It may not include audio. It is ideal for screen captures and recording only part of your screen.

- **Camtasia Studio 8**: For this product, please visit `http://www.techsmith.org`.

  Camtasia is a very robust product with much flexibility. It is possible to produce a very high-quality screen capture and maintain high quality. You can also optimize for different aspect ratios, which is important when thinking about users who may use smartphones and tablets. It is available for Windows and Mac. You can download a free trial.

Producing and sharing presentations

There are many options to include presentations in your course that you can build yourself or embed from other sites.

Audio only

You may be in a situation where you want to create a high-quality audio file and, perhaps later, sync it with your presentation.

This is a good way to avoid poor-quality audio. Having high-quality audio is important if your users are hard of hearing and use assistive speech-to-text software. Even if they do not, it is a good idea to develop a script and an outline for your course to make available when you create a screencast. You will then be following the practices of Universal Design for Learning and also complying with ADA guidelines.

To download and install audio tools, perform the following steps:

1. Download Audacity at `http://audacity.sourceforge.net/`. Audacity is available for both Mac as well as Windows.

2. Select the Audacity installer option since it will guide you through the entire process. If you do not have permissions, you may need to download the ZIP files.

3. In order to convert the AVI files to the MP3 files, you'll need to download an encoder. The LAME MP3 encoder for Windows can be found at `http://lame1.buanzo.com.ar/#lamewindl`.

4. If you have any questions about downloading/installing Audacity or LAME, read the manual at `http://manual.audacityteam.org/o/man/faq_installation_and_plug_ins.html`.

5. To share the audio file, optimize it using MP3 encoder and then upload it to Webspace, or open a site on SoundCloud at `http://www.soundcloud.com`. You can also share audio via YouTube.

Presentation only

As you create your presentation, do not forget to create a script or notes. You can make these available as notes or as a separate file. It is particularly important to do so if your presentation is very graphics intensive and does not include much explanatory text. You can also avoid the temptation to fill the screen with too much text using the following options:

1. You may convert your PowerPoint (or other presentation software) file to a PDF file and then upload it to the server space that you have.

2. You can upload your PDF file to a discussion forum in a Learning Management System (Moodle) or share it in your company's repository (for example, Google Docs).

3. You can upload your presentation to SlideShare at `http://www.slideshare.net/`.

Activities and assessments

As you build your course, you'll need to configure the settings so that they automatically score assessments and allow your students to complete their courses in a self-paced independent study environment. This section describes various activities that are easy to implement because they are easy to create and simple for the learner to follow. These are self-scoring activities.

Choice

The activity **Choice** can be easily configured for self-paced self study. Perform the following steps:

1. On the **Adding a new Choice** page, click on **Activity completion**.

2. Select **Show activity as complete when conditions are met**.

Quiz

Quiz is another good activity to include for automated courses. Now, let's give these new user accounts a course to work on using the following steps:

1. In the **Adding a new Quiz** page, click on **Activity completion**.
2. Select **Show activity as complete when conditions are met**.
3. You may wish to select **Students can manually mark the activity as completed**.

Certificates

Moodle allows you to generate certificates if you have installed the **Certificates** add-on from the Moodle Plugin Library. You can configure them to include the name of the course as well as the student's name, score, and other important information. Certificate is a third-party plugin, and if your Moodle site does not have it, you may need to install it.

Now, add a certificate by performing the following steps:

1. In the **Activities** menu, click on **Certificate**.
2. In the **Adding a new Certificate** page, fill in the required fields.
3. Configure the certificate using the different fields and options.
4. In the **Activity completion** menu, select **Show activity as complete when conditions are met**. The conditions to meet depend on the qualifying scores for "mastery".

Achievement

Moodle provides a wide array of options for self-paced independent study students to demonstrate achievement. We've recommended using certificates and badges because the process of earning, issuing, and displaying them can be automated.

In the case of badges, there is an element of gamification, which encourages students to compete with each other to earn badges and be the best in their respective skill sets and interests. We have discussed badges and certificates and it's useful to review them and remind ourselves that they both motivate, while the course is *in progress* and when it is complete.

Summary

In this chapter, we've learned the best way to develop and configure your course for self-paced independent study, which is ideal for students who want to study at any time, any place, and at their own pace.

We've learned how to configure global settings so that your courses have a consistent look and feel. Then, we moved to the course level and determined the best types of resources and activities for your courses. Then, we discussed how to configure them so that they are automated.

Finally, we looked at ways to motivate students, increase their engagement in the course, and encourage course completion by means of demonstrating achievement first via certificates and then by adding a light element of gamification to your course using badges.

In the next chapter, we will guide you through developing cohort-based courses with teacher-student interaction. We'll take a close look at how to configure your courses and determine which resources, activities, and assessments will be the best fit for your cohort-based courses.

6

Developing Cohort-based Courses with Teacher-student Interaction

In the last chapter, you learned the best way to develop a course in Moodle that will be used for self-directed and self-guided students. In that case, the focus was primarily on creating a course that is very clear, self-explanatory, and easy to follow.

Now, as we turn to other types of courses, you'll find that most of the guidelines you followed in developing courses for independent study also apply to courses that are instructor-led and include groups of students who work together. The group, or the cohort, progresses together, and the advantage of having an individual instructor lies in the fact that he/she can provide guidance and personalized feedback to the students.

In this chapter, you'll learn how to best set up a cohort-based course that allows teacher-student interaction. We'll review the best structure to use and the best combination of plugins, resources, and activities to make sure that your course is very flexible and meets the needs of students and teachers, and also provides behind-the-scenes support, which includes Moodle administrators and instructional designers.

We'll start by looking at the main features of an instructor-led cohort-based course, and keep in mind that the course revolves around instructor communication and guidance along with coordinated student performance.

Then, we'll look at the main sources of student and instructor anxiety. Students in an online course that is guided by an instructor are often most worried about the expectations of the instructor. Further, they want to make sure that they are not going to get lost while looking for the course material and exams, and can perform well in a timely fashion. Instructors want to be able to communicate effectively with students and provide timely and effective feedback on assessments.

In this chapter, we'll discuss the following topics:

- Configuring global settings for instructor-led cohort-based courses
- Modifying the appearance globally, including themes
- Selecting the ideal plugins, activities, resources, and assessments
- Developing different ways for instructors to interact with students
- Organizing course material and activities
- Selecting effective assessments

Characteristics of instructor-led cohort-based courses

The traditional face-to-face college course is a cohort-based course and has a fixed number of students who progress together to complete the course, and they're led by an instructor who guides them and provides feedback and assessments.

Online courses are very similar. The only difference is that there are more ways to communicate with each other, since you're working in an online environment and the students may be working together for one class or a series of classes.

The main characteristics of instructor-led cohort-based courses include the following:

- A common start and end date
- A fixed timeline that keeps all students working together
- Communication with the instructor, who provides guidance and feedback
- Student interaction and collaboration, with a focus on communication
- Assessments with instructor guidance and feedback

It is an interesting fact that most online courses in U.S. higher education are cohort based, and they are regularly compared with face-to-face courses in terms of performance, course completion, and satisfaction.

 You can learn more about online learning in U.S. higher education in the Sloan Consortium's eleventh annual report, *Grade Change: Tracking Online Education in the United States, 2013* at the Sloan-C website at http://sloanconsortium.org/publications/survey/grade-change-2013.

As in the case of self-paced independent study courses, instructor-led cohort-based courses can vary widely in their length, scope, complexity, and goals. In colleges and universities, some can require as few as four weeks to complete. Others, however, focus on 8-week or 16-week semester-long courses. Some organizations may cover the material in four weeks, with four separate weekly milestones (topics or units). Online instructor-led cohort-based courses can be offered by colleges, universities, corporations, not-for-profit organizations, retailers, and other organizations that need to provide educational courses and training.

Benefits and limitations of cohort-based courses in Moodle

Many online courses offered by colleges and universities are set up to mirror the face-to-face arrangement of traditional courses, and follow, more or less, the same philosophy. The focus is on the content that is accessed and discussed by class members in an orderly fashion as the term progresses. Guidance is provided by an instructor who explains the material, provides feedback, and shows the best way to learn and perform so that students can achieve the course goals and outcomes.

The following are the benefits of cohort-based courses:

* They improve communication with peers
* The students have an orderly progression through the resources and activities
* They let the instructor provide proper guidance for performing well and achieving the desired course outcomes
* They are built on a template that can be copied across multiple sections
* They offer a sense of community and connection

While cohort-based courses can be popular and provide support for students, there are a few limitations. Disadvantages of cohort-based courses include:

* There can be slow progress of a student through the course
* There's some inflexibility with respect to assignments and the pace of the course
* There are difficulties in communicating with peers if students are in different time zones and do not have continuous access to the Internet

For many institutions, the benefits of cohort-based courses far outweigh the limitations, and the fact that course shells or templates once built can be copied, archived, and deployed makes it convenient to run many groups at the same time. Although it is true that courses for independent study can be copied and deployed, the user experience is not the same as that in a cohort-based course. In a well-run and successful cohort-based course, students have a feeling of community and support.

Setting up your instructor-led course – global settings

As we mentioned in the introduction, probably the two most important considerations in an instructor-led cohort-based course are the following:

- **Clarity with respect to student performance expectations**: What do I do? When do I do it? Where do I get the materials? How and when am I assessed?

- **Communication with the instructor**: How do I contact my students? How can I provide feedback that they will see in a timely way? How do my students expect me to communicate with them?

We can make sure that we achieve the goals of clarity and communication by selecting a framework that gives us the ability to customize the appearance of the course.

The place to get started is in the **Site administration** menu on the main page. If you expand the menu, you will see two key bullet submenus: **Plugins** and **Appearance**. We will start with **Appearance** because we want to select a theme that will make it easy for us to create clarity and communicate.

Theme selection

As we consider the appearance of our course—the theme we want to use—we need to consider the way that our students are likely to interact in an online environment. Rapid communication with students and the ability to interact and ask questions will help ensure your students feel comfortable and confident.

Essential is a new theme as of Moodle 2.5, and it is uniquely useful for Moodle cohorts because it builds in social networking and you do not have to create a lot of complicated code or handcode **Cascading Style Sheets** (CSS). Instead, the **Essential** theme has a form that allows you to enter values. Keep in mind that it is a third-party plugin theme, and if it is not already installed, the Moodle administrator must install it.

Let's take a look at the following steps in order to get started:

1. From the **ADMINISTRATION** block, in the **Site administration** menu, click on **Appearance**.

2. Click on **Themes**.

3. Click on **Theme selector** to change your theme. Then click on the **Change theme** button.

4. Scroll down until you find the **Essential** theme. Then click on **Use theme** and **Continue**.

5. On the **Theme settings** screen, click on the default selection for all the menu items. Make sure that the **Default: Yes** checkbox is checked for the **Enable device detection** field.

6. Click on the **Save changes** button.

The following screenshot will help you find the **Appearance** submenu:

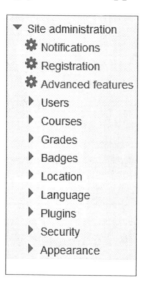

Now, after you've selected the **Essential** theme, you'll have more elements to configure. Notice that in **Themes**, the **Essential** submenu expands to an array of options, which allows you to further customize the appearance of the site.

The following screenshot shows the options of the **Essential** submenu:

Let's expand the **Social Networking** menu and take a look at your options. In your course, you can easily incorporate links to your website, Facebook, Flickr, Twitter, Google+, LinkedIn, Pinterest, Instagram, YouTube, and so on. You can see the **Social Networking** page in the following screenshot:

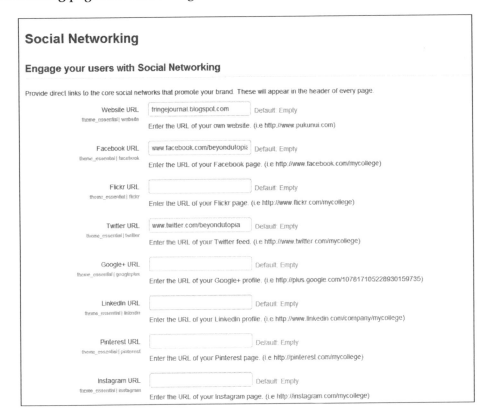

So, any time you have an announcement for students, it is easy to communicate via Moodle and the social networking sites that the students already use regularly. Further, if the students wish to communicate with each other, they can also very easily communicate via Moodle. Using social networking as an extended way to communicate is very helpful when there are questions, the instructor wants to make an announcement, and students wish to communicate with each other, either all at once or with selected individuals (perhaps in collaborative groups). However, there can be risks in incorporating social media in this way because it can be tempting to focus on the social media site and forget to come back to Moodle.

If you select the **Essential** theme as the default theme that all your courses use, and then go to the **General Settings** menu, you'll be able to easily incorporate a site icon, a unique font combination, and your own logo. In addition, you can easily customize the page width, layout, and other information.

You can also track traffic if you click on the **Google Analytics** menu in the navigation bar and check the **Enable Google Analytics** checkbox.

Configuring the plugins

As we configure the courses and set the global settings, let's review the plugins.

Let's make sure that we have configured the plugins so that they are ideal for instructor-led cohort-based courses and that they help us achieve our goals of clarity for students and good communication for instructors.

Course formats

Let's select **Course formats** from the **Plugins** menu in **Site administration**. On the **Manage course formats** page, observe that we've selected the **Topics format** option as the default format. If you have a group, it's often a good idea to select **Weekly format** instead of **Topics format** because you can keep everyone in sync. However, we've selected **Topics format** because this makes it clearer to the students to know that the topics tie to dates in the calendar. Including the topic and the dates in a course prevents ambiguity.

The following screenshot shows the **Manage course formats** page:

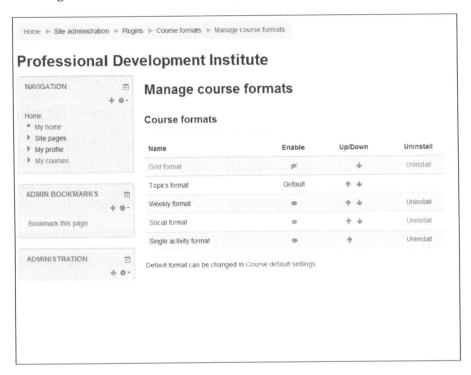

Forum

While we are in the **Site administration** menu, we can easily look at the global settings for our forums so that all the courses have the look, feel, and functionality that is ideal for a cohort-based course. We are at a deciding point because we need to determine how to make sure people know which students are replying to threads, and how people are responding.

Because of the discussions in response to a thread that the instructor has posted and the desire of the students to see peer responses it's best to select a threaded response.

Now, let's take a look at the settings by performing the following steps:

1. In the **Site administration** menu, click on **Plugins**.
2. Click on **Activity modules**.
3. Click on **Forum**.
4. On the **Forum** screen, set the option **Display mode** to **Display replies in threaded form**.

Now, you will configure the option for e-mail address in the reply of the post, specify the length of posts and the number of discussions per page, and indicate the maximum number of attachments that are allowed per post. You may refer to the following screenshot to view the options available on the **Forum** page:

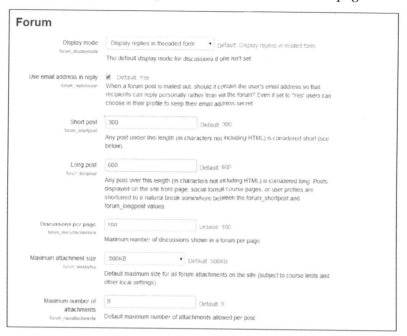

The decisions that you make are important because you'll be using the **Forum** module in all your cohort-based courses for the following items:

- News and announcements
- Questions for the instructor
- Student lounge
- Topic-specific graded discussions
- Topic-specific links to discussions on readings and activities

Planning your forum and configuring it globally will help you make sure that the course is consistent and students and instructors can use it as a very powerful tool to stay on track with the course.

Calendar

The calendar can be the heart and soul of your cohort-based course. It's a place where you can easily tie the topics to the specific launch and due dates for readings, activities, and assessments. You can enter a very detailed list of events or include only the key ones. The best approach is to be sure to include key events, but avoid too much clutter or information that could be distracting.

Let's set up a calendar for a course that lasts a semester, or 16 weeks, using the following steps:

1. Go to the **Site administration** menu.

2. Click on **Appearance**.

3. Click on **Calendar**.

4. On the **Calendar** page, modify **Days to look ahead** to **120** and change the default settings for **Events to Lookahead**.

5. Click on **Save changes**.

We'll revisit many of the global settings as we begin to work on the design of your course. Keep in mind that the sitewide settings are the global default settings and they do not contain the information that is specific to an individual course.

Course-level configuration

Now that you've configured the course at the site level, you will need to configure the elements at the course level and make sure that they are ideal for instructor-led cohort-based courses. So, go to the **Course administration** menu of the **ADMINISTRATION** block.

Course settings

Let's take a look at the course settings. The following are the ideal settings:

1. In the **ADMINISTRATION** block, go to **Course administration**.

2. Click on **Edit settings**.

3. In the **Course format** section, select the **Topics format** menu from the drop-down menu in the **Format** field, and then, add at least two additional topics to the number of sections (in addition to those that will be units in your course). As in the case of the independent study course, you'll use one of the topics for the instructional materials that you'll be using in the entire course. The other topic will include practice tests / exams/ quizzes.

4. In the **Appearance** section, for **Show gradebook to students**, select **Yes** from the drop-down menu.

5. In the **Completion tracking** section, for **Enable completion tracking**, select **Yes** from the drop-down menu.

6. In the **Groups** section, make sure that you include groups. So, select **Visible groups** from the drop-down menu of **Group mode**. After that, click on **Save changes**.

Resources

Organize your resources around your topics. For resources that students will use in the entire course, create a topic and name it `Course Materials`. Other resources can be added to each topic.

Folder

You've already configured your course to contain a specific topic in which you'll include the texts for the entire course. For example, you may include a link to an e-book that will be used as your course textbook. However, let's collect the files used in each topic in a separate folder using the following steps:

1. On your course page, click on **Add a an activity or resource**

2. Select **Folder**.

3. On the **Adding a new Folder** screen, add the name and description.

4. On the **Description** screen, describe the contents and the course topic.

5. Drag-and-drop files to add them to the folder.

6. In the **Completion tracking** section, select **Students can manually mark the activity as completed**, so that students can track their progress.

7. Click on **Save changes**.

Student-created files

In the previous chapter, we discussed the ideal format for files your students will download.

However, how will your students make files and how can they collaborate? There are a number of open source word processing, spreadsheet, and presentation tools, which also allow integrated file sharing.

Word processing, spreadsheet, and presentation tools

There are a number of Microsoft Office-compatible programs that are cloud based and can enable students to create and format documents, upload, share, and collaborate. Some of these are listed as follows:

- **Zoho Docs**: Visit `http://www.zoho.com/docs/` for more information

  Users can create materials such as presentations, documents, and spreadsheets within the cloud-based Zoho Docs. Zoho Docs allows cloud storage and collaboration. They offer a *light* package that is free and at the time of this writing, allows 5 GB of storage.

- **Google Docs**: Visit `http://docs.google.com` for more information

  Students can upload and save documents to Google Drive. They can then edit them using Google's built-in cloud-based editing program, which includes spreadsheet editing as well. If your students wish to create a website or a document in HTML, it is probably best to use Google Sites (`https://sites.google.com/`) rather than Google Docs.

- **OpenOffice**: Visit `http://www.openoffice.org/download/index.html` for more information

  Apache OpenOffice is extremely popular and has a number of useful extensions and dictionaries. It does not come with a platform or space for cloud-based storage and collaboration, so it may be a bit limited for collaboration.

Activities and assessments

As you build your course, you'll need to configure the settings so students can upload assignments and you can provide feedback and update the grades in the gradebook.

Assignment

There is an activity called **Assignment**. **Assignment** can be easily configured so that students can upload files or copy and paste text that you can grade and return. To work with the **Assignment** activity, perform the following steps:

1. On the **Adding a new Assignment** page, click on the **General** section.
2. Fill in the following fields: **Assignment name** and **Description**.
3. Open the **Availability** section and fill in the required fields.

4. Then, in **Submission types**, be sure to select **File submissions** and **Online text**. Selecting **Online text** will allow students to copy and paste text if they do not have a file format that is compatible. You may also wish to include **Online PoodLL** if you want an online audio editor for audio recording submissions by students and you'd like to tie it to a whiteboard for presentations. Remember that this is a third-party plugin and the Moodle administrator must download and install it if it is not already installed.

5. In **Feedback types**, be sure to select **Feedback comments**, and **Feedback files**.

6. There are other fields that give you options. The **Grade** settings are of particular importance because they give you a chance to tie the assignment to the gradebook, set the standard grade points or display of units, and select how you'll grade the activities.

Grades

Your gradebook can be configured in **Site administration**, which controls the look, feel, and functionality of your courses globally.

Now, let's take a look at how we can configure the grade reports within the course by performing the following steps:

1. In the **ADMINISTRATION** block, navigate to **Course administration | Grades**.

2. Now, again in the **ADMINISTRATION** block, click on **Grade administration**.

3. Click on **Course grade settings** and review the settings on its page.

4. Review **Letters** in the **Grade administration** menu to set grade ranges and other settings.

Remember that whether or not an item shows up in the gradebook, the grading criteria for each item is determined when you add graded activities (which include activities such as **Quiz**, **Workshop**, **Forum**, and **Assignment**).

Course backups for cohort-based courses

A simple way to back up or archive courses for the future is to move the courses after they have been taught to a different place in Moodle.

For example, you can move the courses from the current semester or term to a new location in your Moodle installation, link from the front page, and then change the settings so that they are not visible to anyone except administrators.

The courses can then be backed up and purged of any student or instructor information when appropriate and serve as templates or cloneable shells for courses in the future.

Summary

In this chapter, we've learned the best way to develop and configure your course for instructor-led cohorts, which are the most commonly found online courses at colleges and universities. We have chosen cohort-based courses because they are very popular when students are working together on a topic that requires time to develop skills and knowledge. Cohort-based courses are often very useful in a corporation or training organization because they involve individuals who may be working together in teams or across the organization.

We've learned how to configure global settings so that your courses can maintain clarity with respect to what students must study and achieve. We've also looked at how to configure the settings so that your instructors are able to communicate in a number of different ways, given that students may have different social networking preferences and habits. Then, we reviewed the best themes and how to set up the course for maximum functionality. We reviewed how students will work and how to help them take advantage of open source software for the work they will submit both individually and collaboratively.

Finally, we looked at the best ways to set up resources and activities so that students feel comfortable and how to set up forums to encourage student interaction and instructor feedback.

In the next chapter, we will guide you through developing courses that are student centered and include collaborative activities. We'll take a close look at how to configure your courses and determine which resources, activities, and assessments will be the best fit for your collaboration-focused courses.

7
Creating Student-centered Project-based Courses

In *Chapter 6, Developing Cohort-based Courses with Teacher-student Interaction*, we affirmed that when developing courses that are cohort-based and include teacher-student interaction, it's very important to maintain clarity with respect to course organization and also to establish excellent communication.

Similarly, in student-centered project-based courses, it's important to maintain clarity and good communication. It's also important to keep things as straightforward and simple as possible in terms of the activities you'll ask your students to do. After all, it can be complicated and confusing in the online environment if you have too many places to go and things to do at the same time.

In this chapter, you'll learn how to best set up a student-centered project-based course. We'll focus on a few key components you can use for a successful course and also review open source applications that students can use when they collaborate to create documents, audio files, presentations, and videos. Our goal is to help you, as an instructor, administrator, instructional designer, or Moodle support to quickly and easily design and launch courses.

In this chapter, we'll discuss the following topics:

- Configuring global settings for student-centered project-based courses
- Selecting the best theme
- Choosing the best activities and resources
- Ensuring that the activities are connected to the assessments

- Selecting open source applications for students to use when creating collaborative projects
- Configuring the course to allow effective instructor and peer feedback

Characteristics of student-centered project-based courses

The traditional face-to-face college course is a cohort course and has a fixed number of students who progress together to complete it, and they're led by an instructor who guides them and also provides feedback and assessment on student projects.

Online courses can be very similar. The only difference might be that there are more ways to communicate with each other since you're working in an online environment, and the students may be working together for one class or taking a series of classes together.

Here's an example: In order to prepare students to work together in the global, distributed workplace of today, Centennial University's College of Business has built-in collaborative projects in all their online courses. In the Leadership and Strategic Thinking course, for example, students must collaborate to analyze a business situation and create a presentation as well as documents, an audio version, and a video. While it is possible to modify a course shell from a regular instructor-led cohort course, it is a complex process. So, to optimize the experience for the users and improve the course functionality, a new shell is created for all courses so that they are ideal for collaborative projects.

When considering how to configure the course, the Centennial University online team meets with instructors, instructional designers, instructional technologists, and the Moodle administration team. Before they create the shell, they need to review the main attributes.

The main characteristics of student-centered project-based online courses include the following:

- A common start and end date
- A clear timeline, with milestones
- Collaborative activities that involve students working together in groups
- Accessible feedback from peers and instructors
- A space for students to share files and edit each other's files

- Projects that require students to learn new skills and achieve higher standards of quality (audio editing, image editing, incorporating geographic information, and so on)

Student projects can take many forms, or include portfolios. The key feature is that there are many different versions that are built over time and constant review and revision allows one to build on prior knowledge and develop self-awareness.

 You can learn more about learning portfolios in *The Learning Portfolio: Reflective Practice for Improving Student Learning* at http://www.uwstout.edu/soe/profdev/resources/upload/learningportfolio_000.pdf.

The key to success in a student-centered project-based course is performance and interaction between students and the instructor.

Setting up your project-based course – global settings

Let's continue with the case of Centennial University. As the team members discussed how best to create a template that they could use for all courses that have student projects, a few "must-have" elements emerged. The two most important considerations in a student-centered project-based course are the following:

- **Simple structure**: The main focal point needs to be the collaborative space tied to a clear timeline with milestones. Avoid too many distractions such as quizzes and games.
- **Clear communication**: Students should always have a way to ask and answer questions as they work independently or with other members of a collaborative group.

We can make sure that we achieve the goals of clarity and communication by selecting a framework that gives us the ability to customize the appearance of the course.

Course default settings

We have reviewed how to globally manage course default settings, but let's go over it again because there are a few fields that are of particular importance to all student-centered project-based courses.

Let's take a look at how to get started with changing the course settings:

1. From the **ADMINISTRATION** block in the **Site administration** menu, click on **Courses**.

2. Click on **Course default settings**.

3. In **Course format**, select the format **Topics format**.

4. In **Files and uploads**, select **2MB** as the maximum upload size, or select the largest size allowed by your Moodle administrator. You can, however, work with your administrator to allow more storage size if you need it. As a general rule, it's not a bad idea to use a shared cloud drive resource such as Google Drive to house the drafts in order to avoid reducing the performance of the Moodle server.

5. Turn on the **Completion tracking** option by selecting **Yes** in the dropdown.

6. In **Groups,** select **Visible groups** for **Group mode**.

7. Click on the **Save changes** button.

Theme selection

Aardvark is a very popular theme that was rewritten for Moodle 2.5. Its clean appearance makes it a favorite among colleges and universities, and the three-column display gives you a chance to locate the calendar in a separate column and organize the appearance to make things easy to follow.

Aardvark is a responsive theme, which makes it display well on mobile devices, including smart phones and tablets.

Another aspect of Aardvark is the fact that it contains fields that allow you to set up social networking without having to write custom code for CSS.

Let's take a look at how to get started with selecting the Aardvark theme:

1. From the **ADMINISTRATION** block in the **Site administration** menu, click on **Appearance**.

2. Navigate to **Themes | Theme selector**.

3. Click on **Change theme**.

4. Scroll down until you find **Aardvark**. This is not a core theme. If it is not included, you may wish to ask your Moodle administrator to download and install it. An easier solution would be to use the **Clean** theme if Aardvark is not installed. Click on **Use theme** and then click on **Continue** if prompted.

5. In the Moodle **Theme settings** screen, click on the default options for all the menu items. Make sure that the **Default: Yes** checkbox is checked for **Enable device detection**.

6. Click on the **Save changes** button.

To customize the appearance of your course, you may add a logo and/or access to social networking sites for easy communication among your students, using the following steps:

1. From the **ADMINISTRATION** block in the **Site administration** menu, click on **Appearance**.

2. Click on **Themes**.

3. Scroll down until you find **Aardvark**. Click on **Aardvark**. Click on **Change theme**.

4. In **Basic settings**, enter the URL of the logo you'd like to use.

5. In **Social icons**, customize the social network icons you'd like to use by adding the URLs of the social media accounts you'd like to incorporate in their respective text fields. The various social media accounts that are available are as follows:

   ○ **Website URL**

   ○ **Facebook URL**

   ○ **Twitter URL**

   ○ **Google+ URL**

   ○ **Flickr URL**

   ○ **Pinterest URL**

   ○ **Instagram URL**

   ○ **LinkedIn URL**

   ○ **YouTube URL**

   ○ **Apple App Store URL**

   ○ **Google Play Store URL**

6. Click on the **Save changes** button.

 For more information about the Aardvark theme, which includes a description, reviews, and stats, along with a discussion of its issues, please visit Moodle.org's plugins directory at `https://moodle.org/plugins/view.php?plugin=theme_aardvark`.

Some of the social media websites available in **Social Icons** are shown in the following screenshot:

Social Icons

Customise social network icons.

Website URL theme_aardvark | website	http://www.beyondutopia.net	Default: Empty
	Enter the URL of your main website. (i.e http://www.mycollege.ac.uk)	
Facebook URL theme_aardvark | facebook		Default: Empty
	Enter the URL of your Facebook page. (i.e http://www.facebook.com/mycollege)	
Twitter URL theme_aardvark | twitter	@beyondutopia	Default: Empty
	Enter the URL of your Twitter feed. (i.e http://www.twitter.com/mycollege)	
Google+ URL theme_aardvark | googleplus		Default: Empty
	Enter the URL of your Google+ profile. (i.e http://plus.google.com/107817105228930159735)	
Flickr URL theme_aardvark | flickr	flickr.com/beyondutopia	Default: Empty
	Enter the URL of your Flickr page. (i.e http://www.flickr.com/mycollege)	

By enabling social networking, your students can collaborate and connect easily in platforms outside Moodle. Keep in mind that social networking sites such as YouTube allow public and private settings so that students can decide to share their work with the world if they wish to do so or keep it accessible to only a few.

Configuring the workshop settings

Let's select **Activity modules** from the **Plugins** menu in **Site administration** and navigate to **Manage activities | Workshop**.

Now, let's take a look at the settings of workshop. The default settings will probably work well for you, but you may want to pay attention to the following:

- **Maximum submission attachment size**: The default value of this option depends on the site settings and the server settings, and it could be too small for attachments containing audio, video, or a number of images. You may wish to use Google Drive, which allows up to 15 GB of space, or another cloud storage service.

- **Number of reviews**: The default value of this option is usually **5**. You may want more.

Calendar

As in the case of the instructor-led and independent self-study courses, it's critical to set up a calendar that is clear and includes the main project dates along with key milestones and deadlines. Keep in mind that we're configuring global settings, and we're doing it here in order for all our courses to be consistent. We'll set events, such as due dates, within the courses themselves.

Let's set up a calendar for a course that lasts a semester or 16 weeks:

1. Go to the **Site administration** menu.
2. Click on **Appearance**.
3. Click on **Calendar**.
4. On the **Calendar** page, set the **Days to look ahead** value to **90**, and also change the default value for **Events to Lookahead** to **any value**.
5. Click on **Save changes**.

The course-level deadlines and milestones will be set up when you configure the individual course (or your demo course).

Course-level configuration

Now that you've configured your courses at the site level, let's set up a project-based course.

Course settings

First, we will add a course. Remember that we learned how to do that in *Chapter 1, Preparing to Build an Exemplary Moodle Course*, in the **Site administration** menu, where you can add a course by creating it within one of the categories you've created. Navigate to **Courses** in the **Site administration** menu as shown in the following screenshot:

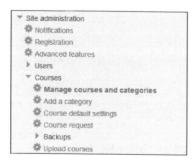

In the **Site administration** menu, perform the following steps:

1. Click on **Manage courses and categories**. The **Course and category management** page appears displaying the **Course categories** list as shown in the following screenshot:

2. Now click on a category and then select **Create new course** as shown in the following screenshot:

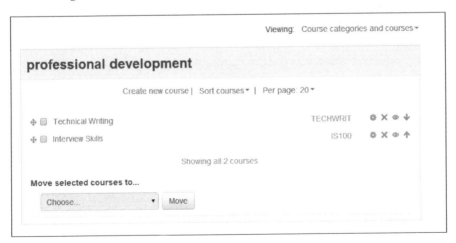

3. On the **Edit course settings** page, enter the mandatory details in the **Course full name** and **Course short name** fields and then click on **Save changes**.

Now we're ready to set up the course so that it will work well for students collaborating on projects. Let's keep it simple to avoid confusion. The following are the ideal settings:

1. In the **ADMINISTRATION** block, go to **Course administration**.
2. Click on **Edit settings**.
3. On the **Edit Course settings** page, select the course format **Topics format**, and then, add at least two additional topics: one for the instructional materials you will use in the course and the other for sample projects and links to open source applications.
4. In the **Appearance** section, set **Show gradebook to students** to Yes.
5. Set **Enable completion tracking** to Yes.
6. Make sure you include groups by selecting **Visible groups** under **Groups | Group mode**.
7. Click on the **Save changes** button.

Providing resources for the course

In previous chapters, we discussed how to set up folders and links to provide resources for your students. For resources that students will use in the entire course, create a topic and name it Course materials.

To include other readings and topic-specific material, add them to each topic.

Links to applications for projects

If your students are creating collaborative presentations, they will need to be able to edit and add audio, video, and text files. They will also need to integrate geographical data.

In previous chapters, we discussed creating links to word-processing, spreadsheet, and presentation tools. Now let's look at open source and free tools for audio and video.

Audio, video, and geographical information tools

The following are a few free, and often open source, tools:

- **Audacity**: Audacity is a wonderful program for creating and editing audio files. You may download and install it on your own computer, and it works on Windows, Mac, and Linux. For more information and to download it, please visit `http://audacity.sourceforge.net/`.

- **LAME**: To convert Audacity projects to MP3 files, you'll need to use an MPEG Audio Layer III (MP3) encoder. LAME is very effective. For more information and to download it, please visit `http://lame.sourceforge.net/`.

- **LibriVox Checker**: LibriVox has made available a program that checks volume. It's extremely useful and easy to use. It also checks file formatting, though this is a feature you may not need to use. For more information, please visit `http://wiki.librivox.org/index.php/Checker`.

- **Google Earth**: Google Earth is probably the easiest and best-known open source Geographical Information System and very helpful for supplying maps and locations for collaborative projects. To see the terms and conditions and to download it, please visit `http://www.google.com/earth/download/ge/agree.html`.

- **YouTube Video Editor**: YouTube's video editor is very easy to use, and it's free. It is not as complicated as other free video editors and does not have controls like those of Camtasia, but it's excellent for collaborations because it's uncomplicated and allows you to add transcripts for compliance with regulations concerned with ensuring that people with disabilities have access to the information being presented. You may upload text or rely on YouTube's built-in speech recognition software, which can be very effective if there is not much background noise. The YouTube video editor is available at `http://www.youtube.com/editor`.

Selecting activities

As we configure the courses and global settings, let's review the activities, which are plugins in Moodle.

The main activities that we will use are forum, workshop, and wiki. Since we already know how to set up a discussion forum, we will not review how to add a forum to a topic. Instead, we'll focus on workshop and wiki.

Activities and assessments

Let's return to the case of Centennial University's courses for their College of Business. The team is now looking at the best ways for students to work collaboratively, which means that they will work together to create and edit files, comment on them, and evaluate them. After reviewing the activities available through Moodle, two were identified as ideal for Centennial's online courses that require collaboration on projects.

The two activities the team members decided on were workshop and wiki. Workshop's ability to let students submit work and then grade their own work and also that of their fellow students was perfect for the university's needs.

Wiki was selected because it allows students to collaborate quickly and easily, and the final results can incorporate collaboratively edited text as well as contributed video, audio, and images from members of the team.

Workshop

Thankfully, the Centennial University team found that building a workshop activity in Moodle courses is easy to do and that it provides a chance for students to create documents, which they then submit and assess. The assessments are reflected directly in gradebook, which appears automatically when the submission is set up. The following steps show you how to get started:

1. Go to the topic that aligns most closely with the one in which you want to place your collaborative project.
2. Go to **Add an activity or resource menu and choose Workshop**.
3. On the **Adding a new Workshop** page, expand **General**.
4. Fill in the following fields: **Workshop name** and **Description**.
5. Open **Submission settings** and fill in the fields for **Instructions for submission** and **Maximum number of submission attachments**, among others.
6. Then, in **Assessment settings**, be sure to fill the field titled **Instructions for assessment**.
7. In **Example submissions**, select the checkbox to allow example submissions for practice in assessing.
8. Keep in mind that most of the fields will be already set as default (which you established while configuring the global settings).

The beauty of a workshop activity is that it allows students to learn from each other and to learn from their mistakes. When they assess their own work or peers' work, they enter comments in accordance with instructions, which can be posted in **Instructions for assessment**. You can enter instructions from **Adding a Workshop** in the **Assessment settings** expandable link, as shown in the following screenshot:

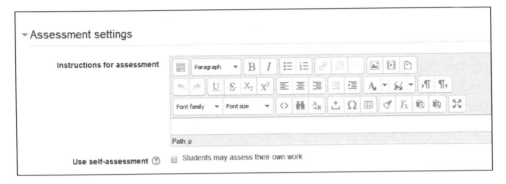

When the students read the comments, they can then apply the suggestions and insights to a revision of the documents that we have created for students to assess. The revision can be submitted as well, which allows more feedback and reflection on one's work and can be enhanced through the **Feedback** expandable link, which allows you to select the number of feedback attachments and the feedback size and write a conclusion that appears in the gradebook as shown in the following screenshot:

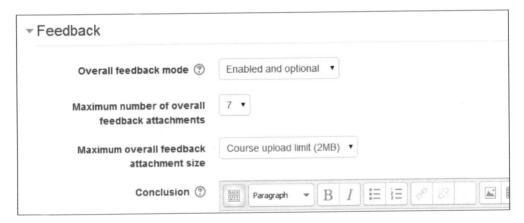

Configuring wiki

The Centennial University College of Business has decided to implement a wiki activity in their courses to help students learn key terms in a way that allows them to interact with fellow students and foster engagement with the course matter. For example, in the Leadership and Strategic Thinking course, students collaborate in a Leadership Theories wiki. All students must post at least one theory and contribute to the definitions of at least 10 theories.

Moodle's wiki activity is ideal for that purpose. Students create HTML documents collaboratively and review each others' additions and changes.

Wikis are good for encouraging students to gain in-depth knowledge on a concept by taking a hands-on, collaborative approach. To get started, go to the topic that aligns most closely to the one in which you want to place your wiki and perform the following steps:

1. In the **Adding a new Wiki** page, expand **General**.
2. Fill in the following fields: **Wiki name** and **Description**.
3. Click on the **Wiki mode** dropdown and select **Collaborative wiki**.
4. Then, in **Common module settings**, set **Visible** to **Show**.
5. Click on the **Save and return to course** button.

Once you have edited the settings in your wiki, you can make it available for students. Students can click on **Edit** and then add, delete, or comment on the entry. To see who has added or deleted content, they can click on **History** and see who has contributed and when. The **Leadership theories** page is shown in the following screenshot:

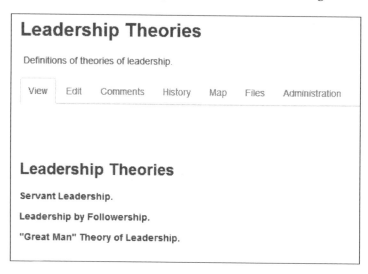

Once the students have finished contributing to wiki, the instructor can grade the activity and determine grades based on the quality and quantity of student contributions. The instructor can click on **Comments** at any time during the process in order to give guidance. If it's done well, wiki can create a wonderful sense of pride and camaraderie and be very motivating as well as informative.

Configuring grades

Your gradebook can be configured in **Course administration**, which controls the look, feel, and functionality course wide.

Now, let's take a look at how we can configure the grade reports within the course:

1. In the **ADMINISTRATION** block, navigate to **Course administration | Grades**.
2. In the **Grade administration** menu, select **Course grade settings** and review the settings. Keep in mind that these settings will automatically populate the gradebook.
3. Click on **Letters** to set grade ranges and other settings.
4. Click on the **Save and return to course** button.

Remember that whether or not an item shows up in the gradebook, the grading criteria for each item is determined when you add graded activities.

Summary

In this chapter, we learned the best way to develop and configure your student-centered project-based courses. We focused on the fact that students will need a very clear structure to manage their projects and that you'll need to provide support in terms of links to applications that they may need in order to perform their collaborative activities.

We looked at the importance of having an easy-to-modify, flexible, responsive theme so that the course has a good look and feel on all devices.

In the next chapter, we will guide you through using Moodle to create online communities, which will use the flexibility of Moodle to develop new ways of training and knowledge transfer.

8
Moodle for Online Communities

Now that you're familiar with the ways to use Moodle for different types of courses, it is time to take a look at how groups of people can come together as an online community and use Moodle to achieve their goals.

For example, individuals who have the same interests and want to discuss and share information in order to transfer knowledge can do so very easily in a Moodle course that has been set up for that purpose.

There are many practical uses of Moodle for online communities. For example, members of an association or employees of a company can come together to achieve a goal and finish a task. In this case, Moodle provides a perfect place to interact, collaborate, and create a final project or achieve a task.

Online communities can also be focused on learning and achievement, and Moodle can be a perfect vehicle for encouraging online communities to support each other to learn, take assessments, and display their certificates and badges. Moodle is also a good platform for a **Massive Open Online Course (MOOC)**.

In this chapter, we'll apply what we've learned in earlier chapters to create flexible Moodle courses that are ideal for online communities and that can be modified easily to create opportunities to harness the power of individuals in many different locations to teach and learn new knowledge and skills.

In this chapter, we'll show you the benefit of Moodle and how to use Moodle for the following online communities and purposes:

- Knowledge-transfer-focused communities
- Task-focused communities
- Communities focused on learning and achievement

Moodle and online communities

It is often easy to think of Moodle as a learning management system that is used primarily by organizations for their students or employees. The community tends to be well defined as it usually consists of students pursuing a common end, employees of a company, or members of an association or society.

However, there are many informal groups and communities that come together because they share interests, the desire to gain knowledge and skills, the need to work together to accomplish tasks, and let people know that they've reached milestones and acquired marketable abilities.

For example, an online community may form around the topic of climate change. The group, which may use social media to communicate with each other, would like to share information and get in touch with like-minded individuals. While it's true that they can connect via Facebook, Twitter, and other social media formats, they may lack a platform that gives a "one-stop shopping" solution. Moodle makes it easy to share documents, videos, maps, graphics, audio files, and presentations. It also allows the users to interact with each other via discussion forums. Because we can use but not control social networks, it's important to be mindful of security issues. For that reason, Moodle administrators may wish to consider ways to back up or duplicate key posts or insights within the Moodle installation that can be preserved and stored.

In another example, individuals may come together to accomplish a specific task. For example, a group of volunteers may come together to organize a 5K run fundraiser for epilepsy awareness. For such a case, Moodle has an array of activities and resources that can make it possible to collaborate in the planning and publicity of the event and even in the creation of post event summary reports and press releases.

Finally, let's consider a person who may wish to ensure that potential employers know the kinds of skills they possess. They can display the certificates they've earned by completing online courses as well as their badges, digital certificates, mentions in high achievers lists, and other gamified evidence of achievement. There are also the MOOCs, which bring together instructional materials, guided group discussions, and automated assessments. With its features and flexibility, Moodle is a perfect platform for MOOCs.

Building a knowledge-based online community

For our knowledge-based online community, let's consider a group of individuals who would like to know more about climate change and its impact. To build a knowledge-based online community, the following are the steps we need to perform:

1. Choose a mobile-friendly theme.
2. Customize the appearance of your site.
3. Select resources and activities.

Moodle makes it possible for people from all locations and affiliations to come together and share information in order to achieve a common objective. We will see how to do this in the following sections.

Choosing the best theme for your knowledge-based Moodle online communities

As many of the users in the community access Moodle using smartphones, tablets, laptops, and desktops, it is a good idea to select a theme that is responsive, which means that it will be automatically formatted in order to display properly on all devices.

 You can learn more about themes for Moodle, review them, find out about the developers, read comments, and then download them at https://moodle.org/plugins/browse. php?list=category&id=3.

There are many good responsive themes, such as the popular **Buckle** theme and the **Clean** theme, that also allow you to customize them. These are the *core* and *contributed* themes, which is to say that they were created by developers and are either part of the Moodle installation or available for free download.

If you have Moodle 2.5 or a later version installed, your installation of Moodle includes many responsive themes. If it does not, you will need to download and install a theme. In order to select an installed theme, perform the following steps:

1. In the **Site administration** menu, click on the **Appearance** menu.
2. Click on **Themes**.
3. Click on **Theme selector**.

4. Click on the **Change theme** button.

5. Review all the themes.

6. Click on the **Use theme** button next to the theme you want to choose and then click on **Continue**.

Using the best settings for knowledge-based Moodle online communities

There are a number of things you can do to customize the appearance of your site so that it is very functional for knowledge-transfer-based Moodle online communities. The following is a brief checklist of items:

- Select **Topics format** under the **Course format** section in the **Course default settings** window. By selecting topics, you'll be able to organize your content around subjects.

- Use the **General** section, which is included as the first topic in all courses. It has the **News forum** link. You can use this for announcements highlighting resources shared by the community.

- Include the name of the main contact along with his/her photograph and a brief biographical sketch in **News forum**. You'll create the sense that there is a real "go-to" person who is helping guide the endeavor.

- Incorporate social media to encourage sharing and dissemination of new information. Brief updates are very effective, so you may consider including a Twitter feed by adding your Twitter account as one of your social media sites.

Even though your main topic of discussion may contain hundreds of subtopics that are of great interest, when you create your Moodle course, it's best to limit the number of subtopics to four or five. If you have too many choices, your users will be too scattered and will not have a chance to connect with each other. Think of your Moodle site as a meeting point. Do you want to have too many breakout sessions and rooms or do you want to have a main networking site? Think of how you would like to encourage users to mingle and interact.

Selecting resources and activities for a knowledge-based Moodle online community

The following are the items to include if you want to configure Moodle such that it is ideal for individuals who have come together to gain knowledge on a specific topic or problem:

1. **Resources**: Be sure to include multiple types of files: documents, videos, audio files, and presentations.

2. **Activities**: Include **Quiz** and other such activities that allow individuals to test their knowledge.

3. **Communication-focused activities**: Set up a discussion forum to enable community members to post their thoughts and respond to each other.

The key to creating an effective Moodle course for knowledge-transfer-based communities is to give the individual members a chance to post critical and useful information, no matter what the format or the size, and to accommodate social networks.

Building a task-based online community

Let's consider a group of individuals who are getting together to plan a fundraising event. They need to plan activities, develop materials, and prepare a final report. Moodle can make it fairly easy for people to work together to plan events, collaborate on the development of materials, and share information for a final report.

Choosing the best theme for your task-based Moodle online communities

If you're using volunteers or people who are using Moodle just for the tasks or completion of tasks, you may have quite a few Moodle "newbies". Since people will be unfamiliar with navigating Moodle and finding the places they need to go, you'll need a theme that is clear, attention-grabbing, and that includes easy-to-follow directions.

There are a few themes that are ideal for collaborations and multiple functional groups. We highly recommend the **Formal white** theme because it is highly customizable from the **Theme settings** page. You can easily customize the background, text colors, logos, font size, font weight, block size, and more, enabling you to create a clear, friendly, and brand-recognizable site.

Formal white is a standard theme, kept up to date, and can be used on many versions of Moodle.

> You can learn more about the **Formal white** theme and download it by visiting `http://docs.moodle.org/26/en/File:theme_ formalwhite.png`.

In order to customize the appearance of your entire site, perform the following steps:

1. In the **Site administration** menu, click on **Appearance**.
2. Click on **Themes**.
3. Click on **Theme settings**.
4. Review all the themes settings.
5. Enter the custom information in each box.

Using the best settings for task-based Moodle online communities

As your users will be working together in groups and collaborating on course projects, there are a few settings that will help accomplish tasks. The following is a brief checklist of those items:

-   Select **Topics format** under the **Course format** section in the **Course default settings** window. You'll be able to organize your content around specific topics by selecting them. If you wish to organize your course around specific tasks, you can use the **Weekly format** menu.
-   Include a calendar block and be sure to add main task deadlines and milestone dates.
-   Enable **Visible Groups** on the **Course default settings** screen to enable setting up groups to work on tasks.
-   Incorporate social media to encourage sharing and disseminating new information. Brief updates are very effective, so you may consider including a Twitter feed.

Make sure that you cluster tasks in a file or topic that you title Main Tasks rather than having a separate topic for each task. Think of the clearest and easiest way to help your users find the tasks (and subtasks) they need to participate in.

Selecting resources and activities for a task-based Moodle online community

The following are the items that could be included in a task-based Moodle site:

1. **Appearance**: Include a calendar block and be sure to include key events and timelines for each task.

2. **Resources**: Include manuals, maps to events, presentations, links to key URLs that provide information about the tasks, the locations, and other key information.

3. **Activities**: Set up a forum for each task to enable community members to post their thoughts and respond to each other; include the **Workshop** or Wiki activity or a portfolio-based program such as Mahara for collaborating on documents. Also, include examples of completed documents.

4. Incorporate synchronous communication such as web conferencing, if necessary, via Skype or BigBlueButton.

5. Incorporate social media and include ways to update and alert group members, including Twitter, Facebook, and YouTube.

The key to creating an effective Moodle course for task-based communities is keeping group members collaborating in a productive and timely fashion.

Building an online community based on learning and achievement

We live in a world where it is increasingly important to be able to demonstrate your knowledge and share your achievements within your personal and professional networks. It is productive and useful for you to be able to let people know the kinds of skills and competencies you possess. Further, gaining more competencies is motivating when you are in a gamified environment.

Creating a certificate course

Making training and professional development available for a group or community of like-minded users will allow individuals to earn credentials in topics that are in demand. They can also take the courses that have a reputation for high quality, relevant content, and reliable assessment.

The following is a checklist of configurations, settings, and items to include in your certificate course:

- Select the **Essential** theme because it allows you to directly input social networking URLs in the spaces provided on the **Theme Settings** screen. Please note that the **Essential** theme is a contributed theme and if it is not already installed, your Moodle administrator will need to download and install it.

- Create resources such as **Book** for course content, clear presentations/videos, and training material.

- Create your assessment in the form of a self-scored **Quiz** activity.

- On the **Course default settings** screen, enable completion tracking. Make sure that this option has been enabled in the **Advanced features** submenu of the **Site administration** menu.

- Clicking on the **Add an activity or resource** link, add **Certificate**. Configure the certificate's **Activity completion** section so that it shows activity as complete when conditions (certain grade or conditions) are met. Completing the course triggers the generation of a certificate.

- Design certificates that are unique, attractive, descriptive, and that help build your brand. Include your logo and a custom watermark.

- Display the full series of certificates that are available in order to motivate users to earn all of them.

Creating badge-generating courses

Earning badges upon completion of a level or a course and then displaying them in a cloud-based location as well as on Facebook or other social media sites is just one popular example of the "gamification" of training. "Gamifying" training helps one motivate learners because, as in the case of video games, one can display their competency as they ascend to different "levels". Follow the same steps covered in the previous section to create a certificate-generating course. Then continue with the following steps:

1. In the **Site administration** menu, click on **Badges**.
2. Click on **Manage badges** and then click on the **Add a new badge** button.
3. After creating a badge, configure the badge's **Criteria** tab so that it generates a badge upon completion of the course.
4. Design badges that are unique, attractive, descriptive, and that help build your brand.

5. Display the full series of badges that are available in order to motivate users to earn all of them. One good place to do so is in **News forum**, where you can upload a graphic to an icon or a link to a website that includes information about the badge and a graphic for each icon.

6. To give your badge publicity and share it, you may wish to register the ones you offer at the Open Badges project at http://openbadges.org/.

 You can learn more about the Mozilla OpenBadges project and the Mozilla OpenBadges Backpack at http://openbadges.org/.

As you develop your social media publicity strategy, you may wish to feature the testimonials of individuals who have completed courses and display their faces next to their badges. You'll need to obtain permission to use their quotes and images, but it's painless and completely worth the effort. To do so, follow the given procedure:

1. Go go the **Site administration** menu.

2. Click on **Plugins** and **Authentication**.

3. To set permissions and access levels, fill in the fields for **Site policies** by navigating to **Site administration | Security**. Keep in mind that any information you share via a social networking site could be shared or made public.

Creating a MOOC

MOOCs are a great way to offer courses and content to potentially large groups and develop a social network that will do a lot to publicize you and your courses/programs.

You can create a MOOC very easily by simply creating a certificate or custom course and adding groups so that you can facilitate discussions. Create the course in the usual way and simply add a forum for a key topic. You may still base assessments on the self-graded quizzes that, when successfully completed, trigger the generation of a certificate or a badge.

Summary

In this chapter, we've learned the best way to use Moodle to meet the evolving needs of online users. Specifically, we looked at the way in which we can use Moodle's capabilities to help online communities accomplish what they would like to with respect to transferring knowledge and skills, completing collaborative tasks, and demonstrating achievements via social media. In doing so, we've explored Moodle's flexibility and its wide range of core and contributed themes, activities, resources, and plugins.

In this book, we have guided you through the best ways to use Moodle and included information on using Moodle for a wide array of institutions as well as users/learners. We have described the best ways to set up courses and how to select the resources, activities, and assessments for many different uses. Then, we discussed the best ways to structure courses for different purposes, ranging from large cohort courses to self-study courses taken by students individually. Finally, we've explored ways to expand the uses of Moodle to accommodate and embrace new technologies and ways of envisioning knowledge transfer and building skills.

Index

D

Description, course
files, uploading with Course summary files
box 29
typing, in Course summary box 29

F

File resource
adding 42
using, for adding resources 59
Files and uploads section
file size, deciding 33
filters
activating 10
filters, activating
Activity names auto-linking filter 11
Glossary auto-linking filter 12
Multimedia plugins filter 12
folder resource
adding 42
fonts
used, for customizing course appearance 36
Forum activity
adding 44
forum settings
configuring, for cohort-based courses 72, 73
free open source tools
Audacity 88
Google Earth 88
LAME 88
LibriVox Checker 88
YouTube Video Editor 88

G

General menu
settings, configuring 29
**global settings, instructor-led cohort-based
courses**
calendar 74
course formats 71
forums 72, 73
plugins, configuring 71
theme selection 68-71

**global settings, self-paced independent
study courses**
activities, customizing 54-56
calendar, creating 56
configuring 52
theme, selecting 53
Google Docs
URL 76
gradebook
configuring 92
Groups option 34
Guest access option 33

H

Higher Education Opportunity Act, 2008
principles 19
URL 19

I

images
used, for customizing course appearance 36
Instructor/institution links
adding 35
instructor-led cohort-based courses
benefits 67
characteristics 66, 67
limitations 67
setting up 68

J

Jing
URL 61

K

knowledge-based online community
activities, selecting for 97
best settings, using 96
building 95
resources, selecting for 97
theme, choosing for 95

Moodle 2.5 Multimedia Cookbook

ISBN: 978-1-78328-937-0   Paperback: 300 pages

75 recipes to help you integrate different multimedia resources into your Moodle courses to make them more interactive

1. Add all sorts of multimedia features to your Moodle course.

2. Lots of easy-to-follow, step-by-step recipes.

3. Work with sound, audio, and animation to make your course even more interactive.

Moodle for Mobile Learning

ISBN: 978-1-78216-438-8   Paperback: 234 pages

Connect, communicate, and promote collaboration with your coursework using Moodle

1. Adopts practical ideas for demonstrating how to implement mobile learning with Moodle.

2. Empowers you to apply mobile learning in your profession.

3. Discover how other organizations have achieved mobile learning success.

4. Filled with practical and hands-on tutorials for learning practitioners.

Please check **www.PacktPub.com** for information on our titles

[PACKT] open source✣
PUBLISHING   community experience distilled

Moodle JavaScript
Cookbook

Over 50 recipes for making your Moodle system more dynamic
and responsive with JavaScript

Alastair Hole   [   ] open source

Moodle JavaScript Cookbook

ISBN: 978-1-84951-190-2   Paperback: 180 pages

Over 50 recipes for making your Moodle system more
dynamic and responsive with JavaScript

1. Learn why, where, and how to add JavaScript
   to your Moodle site.

2. Get the most out of Moodle's built-in extra—the
   Yahoo! User Interface Library (YUI).

3. Explore a wide range of modern interactive
   features, from AJAX to Animation.

4. Integrate external libraries like jQuery
   framework with Moodle.

Moodle Gradebook

Set up and customize the gradebook to track student progress
through Moodle

Rebecca Barrington   [PACKT] open source

Moodle Gradebook

ISBN: 978-1-84951-814-7   Paperback: 128 pages

Set up and customize the gradebook to track student
progress through Moodle

1. Use Moodle's powerful gradebook more
   effectively to monitor and report on the
   progress of your students.

2. Customize the gradebook to calculate and show
   the information you need.

3. Discover new grading features and tracking
   functions now available in Moodle 2.

Please check **www.PacktPub.com** for information on our titles

Made in the USA
Lexington, KY
25 February 2015